DAN DOHERTY
Cooking at Home

DAN DOHERTY
Cooking at Home

PCC free book outside near the stairs
2-19-2019

MITCHELL BEAZLEY

To Becs, Tilly & Miso. It was a long year, but we got there...
Thank you for being so patient x

An Hachette UK Company
www.hachette.co.uk

First published in Great Britain in 2019 by Mitchell Beazley,
an imprint of Octopus Publishing Group Ltd
Carmelite House
50 Victoria Embankment
London EC4Y 0DZ
www.octopusbooks.co.uk

Distributed in the US by Hachette Book Group
1290 Avenue of the Americas
4th and 5th Floors
New York, NY 10104
www.octopusbooksusa.com

Distributed in Canada by Canadian Manda Group
664 Annette St., Toronto, Ontario, Canada M6S 2C8

ISBN 978 1 78472 559 4

A CIP catalogue record for this book is available from the British Library.

Printed and bound in China

10 9 8 7 6 5 4 3 2 1

Photographer: Dan Jones
Food Stylists: Dan Doherty & Natalie Thomson
Props Stylist: Linda Berlin

Publisher: Alison Starling
Managing Editor: Sybella Stephens
Copy Editor: Jo Richardson
Art Director: Juliette Norsworthy
Senior Production Controller: Allison Gonsalves

PUBLISHER'S NOTES
Both Imperial and metric measurements have been given in all recipes. Use one set of
measurements only and not a mixture of both.

Eggs should be medium and butter should be unsalted, unless otherwise stated.

Oven temperatures given are for fan-assisted ovens. Follow the manufacturer's instructions
for adjusting the time and the temperature if using a non-fan-assisted oven.

Contents

INTRODUCTION

Cooking for a living has been my life for almost 20 years. I moved to London when I was 16 to do my apprenticeship, and have been here ever since. During that time, I've worked in Michelin-starred restaurants, gastro pubs and brasserie-style joints. At the beginning it was important to learn the trade, which is all-encompassing and therefore leaves little time for anything else. While one doesn't stop learning, you do start to find time for other things as you progress through your career, and for me, one of those things was cooking. This may seem a bit odd after spending so long doing it for work, but what I mean specifically is home cooking. It's a totally different matter in my eyes, and something that's incredibly rewarding.

Over the last few years I've found cooking at home more and more enjoyable. I find it relaxes me and allows me to cook without the pressures and responsibilities that being in a restaurant kitchen brings. I don't mean cooking fancy dinners on a Saturday night either; I recently became a dad and found the best way to help Becs while she's dealing with the sometimes constant feeding and healing post-birth was to nourish her with great-tasting food. Now my daughter Tilly is eating, too, and it's lots of fun. We try to eat together, as a family, which is very important to me.

I really enjoy the day-to-day cooking for the family, but I also love having people over for a chilled dinner or a slap-up feast, for a roast or for breakfast. It's fun, social and when you've got kids it's sometimes easier logistically than going out to eat. Cooking at home – the whole idea of home and what that means – is what I care deeply about, so I wanted to share my recipes for all types of occasions. I think there's something here for everyone and every event, too. There are plenty of dips for an easy Friday-night snack in front of the TV or casual get-togethers, one-pot wonders to make life easy, and simple lunch box ideas that are packed with flavour. There are also some of my favourite breakfasts that are perfect for a weekend gathering, plus lots of snacks and nibbles for informal grazing. On top of that there are plenty of side dishes, killer desserts and elaborate feasts to share with the people you love.

Seasonal cooking is a subject I'm really passionate about, too, and one that is ingrained in chefs at my restaurant. As part of writing this book I've created some menus for all the seasons with brilliant dishes that go really well together and celebrate the amazing seasonal produce available. These recipes are a little more involved, but still totally achievable and are perfect for dinner parties.

However busy I am professionally, home cooking is something I continue to do a lot because it makes me happy and because I know my family are getting proper, tasty, nourishing food. I can't wait until Tilly is older and we can teach her about food and how important it is to eat a varied, balanced diet... and of course how to cook! She has a healthy appetite already, so I know it'll be fun. And that's what food should be – fun. Food should be a pleasure to cook and rewarding to feed to others, without being overly complicated or fussy.

This book was really easy to write and a total pleasure to put together; it's an honest collection of the dishes I regularly cook at home – they've been made so many times at my house, I just know the recipes work a treat and, importantly, taste great.

I'm so excited to share my recipes and hope you get as much joy out of them as I do.

MAKES 2 BOWLS

Preparation time 5 minutes
Cooking time 5 minutes

I like to blitz the oats so there is less texture coming from them, and instead use the coconut flakes for a lovely bite – the oats cook much more quickly, too.

Coconut, banana & peanut butter porridge

75g (2¾oz) rolled oats
200ml (7fl oz) almond milk
1 banana
2 tablespoons chunky peanut butter
75g (2¾oz) unsweetened coconut flakes

Put the oats in a food processor and blitz to a powder.

Mix the oat powder with the almond milk in a saucepan. Bring to the boil, stirring occasionally, then reduce the heat and simmer for 5 minutes.

Meanwhile, peel the banana and halve it lengthways. Cut lengthways again into quarters, then chop into 1cm (½-inch) pieces. Reserve a handful to garnish.

When the porridge is ready, stir in the peanut butter, the banana and half the coconut.

Serve in bowls, sprinkling the rest of the coconut and banana on top.

Preparation time 30 minutes, plus
chilling and rising
Cooking time 15 minutes

A little breakfast dessert is a sure-fire way to finish brunch off with a bang! Use your favourite cereal or mix a couple together; it adds a great crunch.

Cereal-crusted glazed doughnuts

500g (1lb 2oz) strong white flour

50g (1¾oz) caster sugar

7g (¼oz) dried active yeast

4 eggs

seeds from 1 vanilla pod

10g (¼oz) sea salt flakes

125g (4½oz) butter, softened, plus extra for greasing

vegetable or sunflower oil, for deep-frying

cereal of your choice, for topping

GLAZE

240g (8½oz) icing sugar, sifted

seeds from 3 vanilla pods

pinch of sea salt flakes

3 tablespoons milk, or more if needed

food colouring, if you fancy

FILLING

400ml (14fl oz) double cream

200g (7oz) cream cheese

200g (7oz) icing sugar, sifted

Using a stand mixer fitted with the dough hook, mix together the flour, sugar, yeast, eggs, vanilla seeds and salt.

While mixing on a medium speed, add enough cold water to form a dough. Continue to mix for 10 minutes.

Reduce the speed to slow, then gradually add the butter. Increase the speed to high until the dough looks stretchy – about 5 minutes.

Turn off the machine and transfer the dough to a bowl. Cover and chill in the refrigerator overnight.

The next day, roll the dough into golf ball-sized balls and place on a baking sheet greased with butter. Cover loosely in clingfilm and leave to rise until doubled in size – about 3 hours.

Heat the oil for deep-frying in a deep-fat fryer or a deep saucepan to 170°C (340°F) – if you don't have a jam thermometer, test if the oil is hot enough by carefully dropping a pinch of dough into the oil; if it sizzles immediately the oil is ready. Fry the balls, in batches of 3–4 at a time, for 2–3 minutes on each side. Remove with a slotted spoon straight on to kitchen paper to drain the excess oil. Let them cool.

To make the glaze, whisk all the ingredients together in a mixing bowl. If it seems a little thick, add a splash more milk. If using multiple colours, divide the mix into separate bowls and stir a few drops of food colouring into each.

To make the filling, in another bowl, whisk the ingredients together until smooth, then transfer to a piping bag.

When the doughnuts are completely cold, make a small cut in the side and pipe some of the filling mixture inside.

Dip the doughnuts in the glaze, then sprinkle a good handful of your favourite cereal on top. Leave to set before serving.

MAKES 3–4

Preparation time 5 minutes,
plus cooling
Cooking time 15 minutes

Using frozen berries is both cost-effective and convenient. If you have fresh berries, they are great, too, but there is no need to cook them – just make the pots up with the fresh fruit and they will taste perfect.

Summer berry compote yogurt pots with honey oats

COMPOTE
(MAKES 200G/7OZ)

250g (9oz) mixed frozen summer berries

1 star anise

1 cinnamon stick

1 tablespoon sugar

HONEY OATS
(MAKES 100G/3½OZ)

2 tablespoons honey

100g (3½oz) rolled oats

pinch of sea salt flakes

500ml (1lb 2oz) full-fat Greek yogurt, to serve

To make the compote, pop all the ingredients into a saucepan and simmer over a low heat for 15 minutes until the water from the berries has evaporated.

Pick out the star anise and cinnamon and let the compote cool. You can store the compote in the refrigerator for 1 week or so.

Meanwhile, to make the honey oats, heat a nonstick frying pan over a medium heat and add the honey. When it starts to bubble, add the oats and caramelize them until golden all over – about 10 minutes. You will need to stir them often. Add the salt at the end, then let the oats cool.

To make up the yogurt pots, layer about 2 tablespoons of yogurt in the base of each pot, top with 1 tablespoon of the compote and then sprinkle with 1 tablespoon of the honey oats. Repeat until you get to the top. If you have glass pots you can use, that's even better, as you can see the colourful layers.

Store any leftover oats in an airtight container for up to 1 month.

MAKES 12

Preparation time 15 minutes
Cooking time 1¾ hours, or 15 minutes
if using precooked sweet potatoes

I love how light this recipe is, and it's really quick if you have some cooked sweet potato left over from the day before.

Sweet potato pancakes with ricotta, pine nuts & honey

1 sweet potato
150g (5½oz) self-raising flour
4 eggs, separated
150ml (5fl oz) milk
pinch of sea salt flakes
knob of butter

TO SERVE
2 large tablespoons ricotta cheese
2 tablespoons good-quality clear honey
30g (1oz) pine nuts, toasted
pinch of sea salt flakes

If making from scratch, preheat the oven to 170°C fan (375°F), Gas Mark 5. If using leftover cooked sweet potato, skip to the blending step and take it from there.

Pierce the sweet potato and wrap in foil. Bake for 1½ hours until cooked through.

Remove the sweet potato from the oven and let it cool enough to handle, then peel.

Add the sweet potato flesh to a food processor and blend to a smooth purée (or use a fork if you don't have a food processor), then transfer to a mixing bowl.

Add the flour, egg yolks and milk to the sweet potato purée and whisk together until smooth.

In another bowl, whisk the egg whites with the salt until stiff, then fold into the pancake mixture.

Heat half the butter in a nonstick frying pan over a medium heat. When melted and bubbling, add 3 separate ladles of the pancake mixture, making 3 x 7.5cm (3-inch) pancakes. Cook for 3 minutes, then flip and cook for the same time on the other sides.

Remove from the pan on to a plate, while you cook the remaining pancake mixture in the rest of the butter in the same way.

To serve, spoon over the ricotta and drizzle over the honey. Finish with a sprinkling of pine nuts all over and the salt.

I love making these cheesy bacon scones, whether to enjoy on their own or to serve alongside a cooked breakfast. You can make the dough the day before and, after rolling, pop in the refrigerator to rest and cook the following morning.

Cheese & bacon scones

100g (3½oz) pancetta or streaky bacon cut into 5mm (¼-inch) pieces

5g (⅛oz) fresh yeast, or 1 x 7g sachet fast-action dried yeast

2 tablespoons water

pinch of caster sugar (if using dried yeast)

150g (5½oz) plain flour, plus extra for dusting

75g (2¾oz) butter, softened

50g (1¾oz) Parmesan cheese, grated

25g (1oz) Cheddar cheese, grated

10g (¼oz) chives, finely chopped

pinch of sea salt flakes

50g (1¾oz) crème fraîche

2 egg yolks

1 egg, beaten, to glaze

Preheat an oven to 180°C fan (400°F), Gas Mark 6. Line a baking sheet with baking paper.

Sauté the pancetta or bacon in a frying pan over a medium heat until golden brown. Remove from the pan straight on to kitchen paper to drain the excess fat. Let it cool.

In a small bowl, mix the fresh (or dried) yeast with 1 tablespoon water. If using dried yeast, also add a pinch of sugar. Stir to dissolve and set aside.

Put the flour in the bowl of a stand mixer fitted with a dough hook. Rub the butter into the flour using your fingertips, then add the Parmesan, half the Cheddar, the chives, salt, pancetta or bacon and yeast mixture. Using a dough hook, mix on a medium speed until well combined. Add the crème fraîche and egg yolks and mix together on a low speed until a dough forms. If the mixture seems dry, add the remaining 1 tablespoon of water. If you don't have a stand mixer, mix the ingredients in a large bowl and knead by hand until the dough comes together.

Roll out the dough on to a generously floured work surface until 4cm (1½-inches) thick, then cut out rounds with a 6cm (2½-inch) diameter cutter. Gather the trimmings together, reroll and continue cutting out rounds until all the dough has been used up.

Put the scones on the lined baking sheet. Brush each one with the beaten egg, then sprinkle the rest of the grated Cheddar over the top. Bake for 15 minutes until golden brown.

Remove from the oven and transfer to a wire rack to cool.

This is a lovely brunch-time dish, especially if you love smoked fish. The prosecco gives a nice subtle flavour that works really well with the smoky haddock and, once the bottle is open, you may as well have a glass to go with!

Smoked haddock, poached egg & prosecco cream

25g (1oz) butter
1 shallot, finely chopped
1 bay leaf
1 glass of prosecco
200ml (7fl oz) double cream
splash of white wine vinegar
2 handfuls of baby spinach, washed
2 smoked haddock fillets, about 125g (4½oz) each, skinned
2 eggs
a few sprigs of basil, leaves chopped
sea salt flakes and freshly ground black pepper

Put half the butter in a saucepan over a low heat and sweat the shallot with the bay leaf for 3–4 minutes until soft but not coloured. Season with salt, but less than you would normally use, as the haddock will be naturally salty.

Add the prosecco, increase the heat and boil until reduced by half, then add the cream and reduce that by half, too.

Strain the cream mixture through a sieve into a clean pan and set aside over a low heat.

For poaching the eggs, bring a pan of water to the boil and add the vinegar.

Meanwhile, melt the remaining butter in a frying pan and sauté the spinach over a medium heat until wilted, then season with salt and pepper. Set aside until ready to serve.

Drop the haddock fillets into the cream and simmer for 4–5 minutes until cooked – the flesh should just fall apart when pressed (they may take less time to cook if the fillets are thin).

While the fish is cooking, gently poach the eggs. Make sure your cooking water is just below simmering, then crack the eggs into a ramekin and lower each one into the water, letting the egg slip out at the last moment. For soft eggs, 3 minutes should be fine; 4–5 minutes if you want the yolks firmer. When cooked to your liking, remove with a slotted spoon and place on kitchen paper to absorb the water.

Add the basil to the creamy haddock sauce.

To serve, make a nest of the sautéed spinach on each warmed plate. Add a haddock fillet on top of each, then top with a poached egg. Pour over the sauce, then serve.

This is a great dish that's so easy to put together. I use shop-bought tortillas and tomato chilli jam, as it makes the dish super-quick, and it really hits the spot.

Quesadillas with tomato chilli jam, bacon, cheese & fried eggs

8 streaky bacon rashers

2 soft corn tortillas

4 tablespoons tomato chilli jam

4 slices of aged Cheddar cheese

knob of butter

vegetable oil, for frying the eggs

2 eggs

Grill the bacon rashers until nice and crisp, then let them cool on kitchen paper.

Preheat an oven to 180°C fan (400°F), Gas Mark 6.

Spread one of the tortillas with half the tomato chilli jam. Add half the bacon, then half the cheese on top and fold it in half. Repeat to make a second quesadilla.

Heat a large ovenproof frying pan over a medium heat. Add the knob of butter and wait until it starts to foam slightly, then add the quesadillas and cook for 3–4 minutes until golden brown. Turn over and cook on the other side in the same way.

Transfer the pan to the oven for 5 minutes while you fry the eggs. Heat another frying pan over a medium heat and add some vegetable oil. Crack the eggs into the pan and gently fry for 3–4 minutes until cooked but still with soft yolks.

Remove the quesadilla from the oven, cut in half and put on to 2 plates. Top each serving with a fried egg and eat straight away.

This isn't a proper frittata because I don't whisk up the eggs, as is done traditionally, since I want a runny yolk here. But it's the same process; I just fry the eggs around the ingredients rather than combine them all together.

Spring vegetable "frittata"

olive oil, for cooking and drizzling

1 leek, trimmed, cleaned and finely sliced into rounds 5mm (¼-inch) thick

2 handfuls of fresh peas

8 asparagus spears, woody ends removed, cut into 2cm (¾-inch) pieces

4 eggs

20g (¾oz) Parmesan cheese

pinch of chilli flakes

1 lemon

½ bunch (about 15g/½oz) basil leaves

sea salt flakes and freshly ground black pepper

Heat some olive oil in a flameproof dish or large frying pan over a medium heat. Add the leek and sweat, without colouring, for a few minutes. Season with salt and pepper.

Add the peas and asparagus and sauté for a further 3–4 minutes.

Using a spoon or spatula, make 4 little wells in the pan for the eggs to be cracked into. Crack in the eggs and gently fry for 3–4 minutes or until the whites are set and the yolks are still runny. In the last few moments before the eggs are set, finely grate the Parmesan over and cover with a lid to finish cooking the eggs, keeping the yolks nice and soft.

When ready, take the lid off and turn off the heat. Finish the pan of eggs with a drizzle of olive oil, the chilli flakes and the lemon zested over. Tear over the basil leaves and serve.

Preparation time 15 minutes
Cooking time 10 minutes, or 1½ hours
if making the chutney

This recipe makes me think of alfresco breakfasts in the garden; the flavours are so fresh and light. I've added my recipe for tomato chutney, but good-quality shop bought is perfectly fine, too.

Spicy sweetcorn fritters with tomato chutney

100g (3½oz) self-raising flour

2 eggs, beaten

100ml (3½fl oz) milk

1 tablespoon soured cream

2 x 198g (7oz) cans of sweetcorn kernels, drained

2 spring onions, finely chopped

a few sprigs of coriander, leaves and stems finely chopped

1 red chilli, finely chopped

½ teaspoon ground cumin

finely grated zest and juice of 1 lime

sea salt flakes and freshly ground black pepper

vegetable oil, for cooking

CHUTNEY (MAKES 2 JAM JARS)

2 red onions, finely chopped

8 tomatoes, chopped into 2cm (¾-inch) chunks

3 garlic cloves, finely chopped

1 red chilli, finely chopped

1 star anise

1 tablespoon fennel seeds

200g (7oz) caster sugar

150ml (5fl oz) sherry vinegar

TO SERVE

4 tablespoons soured cream

a few sprigs of coriander, leaves roughly chopped

To make the chutney, put all the ingredients in a large stainless steel pan and bring to a simmer. Cook, without a lid on, for about 1½ hours until all the liquid has reduced and the mixture has started to caramelize. Spoon into sterilized jars, seal and store in a cool, dark place. It will keep for up to 1 week, or unopened for up to 1 month.

To make the fritters, put the flour in a mixing bowl and make a well in the middle. Add the eggs, milk and soured cream to the well, then gradually whisk the flour into the wet ingredients to make a batter.

Add all the other ingredients (except the vegetable oil for cooking) and season with salt and pepper.

Heat a nonstick frying pan over a medium heat and drizzle with oil. Spoon 3 separate large dollops of the batter (about half the total amount) into the pan and cook for 2–3 minutes on each side until golden brown and cooked through.

Remove from the pan on to a wire rack and season with salt. Repeat with the rest of the batter.

To serve, top each fritter with a spoon of soured cream and chutney, and finish with some coriander leaves sprinkled on top.

I've only recently started cooking this and now I can't get enough. I've always been a big fan of spicy foods to cure a hangover, and this is the perfect breakfast for the morning after the night before.

Masala "recovery" scrambled eggs

4 eggs

knob of butter

1 onion, finely chopped

1 garlic clove, finely chopped

1 small bird's eye chilli, finely chopped (leave the seeds in if you like it really spicy)

1 teaspoon ground cumin

1 teaspoon ground turmeric

1 teaspoon masala curry powder

splash of double cream (optional)

about 10g (½oz) coriander, leaves and stems chopped

sea salt flakes and freshly ground black pepper

well-buttered toast, to serve

Beat the eggs together in a mixing bowl, and season with salt and pepper.

Heat the butter in a frying pan over a medium heat. When it begins to bubble, add the onion, garlic and chilli and cook for 3–4 minutes until softened but not coloured.

Add the cumin, turmeric and curry powder and cook for a further 3–4 minutes.

Add the beaten eggs and reduce the heat to low. Cook, stirring all the time, until the eggs are scrambled. If using the cream, add at the end of cooking and stir in.

Finally, stir in the chopped coriander and serve with buttery toast.

I make this at least once a week, especially in winter. I find the spice so healing and it sets you up well for a cold day ahead.

Curried chickpea & tomato baked eggs

olive oil, for cooking

½ onion, finely chopped

2 garlic cloves, finely chopped

1 bay leaf

1 red chilli, finely chopped

1 teaspoon cumin seeds, toasted

1 tablespoon Madras curry powder

pinch of cayenne pepper

1 red pepper, cored, deseeded and sliced 5mm (¼-inch) thick

400g (14oz) can of chopped tomatoes

400g (14oz) can of chickpeas, drained and rinsed

200ml (7fl oz) vegetable stock

½ small bunch (about 15g/½oz) coriander, leaves and stems finely chopped, reserving a handful for garnish

a few sprigs of flat leaf parsley, finely chopped

a few sprigs of mint, leaves chopped

4 eggs

sea salt flakes and freshly ground black pepper

sourdough bread, toasted

Put some olive oil in a pan over a medium heat and sauté the onion, garlic, bay leaf and chilli together for 3 minutes – a little colour is OK. Season with salt and pepper.

Add the cumin, curry powder and cayenne and cook for a further 3 minutes.

Add the red pepper, pop a lid on the pan and cook for 5 minutes until they begin to soften.

Remove the lid, add the chopped tomatoes, chickpeas and the stock, then reduce the heat and simmer for 15 minutes.

Add the coriander, parsley and mint and stir in, then make 4 little wells in the pan for the eggs. Crack in the eggs and simmer over a very low heat for 10 minutes until the eggs are set but still soft, covering with the lid for the last minute to set the top of the eggs. Serve on top of toasted sourdough with extra coriander scattered over.

Lunch boxes

This is a really simple and healthy lunch recipe that can use any veggies alongside or instead of the beetroot.

Middle Eastern mixed grains with beetroot, feta & herbs

100ml (3½fl oz) olive oil

2 onions, finely chopped

2 garlic cloves, finely chopped

1 sprig of rosemary

1 teaspoon ground cumin

1 teaspoon ground coriander

pinch of chilli flakes

100g (3½oz) cooked, ready-to-eat bulgur wheat

100g (3½oz) cooked, ready-to-eat Puy lentils

100g (3½oz) feta cheese, crumbled

a few sprigs of dill, leaves and stems finely chopped

a few sprigs of flat leaf parsley, leaves finely chopped

a few sprigs of mint, leaves finely chopped

juice of 1 lemon

4 cooked beetroots, peeled and cut into 1cm (½-inch) dice

12 cherry tomatoes, quartered

sea salt flakes and freshly ground black pepper

Put a splash of the olive oil in a frying pan over a medium heat and sauté the onions, garlic and rosemary for 4–5 minutes until softened.

Add the cumin, coriander and chilli flakes and cook for a further 3 minutes.

Remove the pan from the heat, add the bulgur wheat and lentils and stir in.

Next, add the feta, all the herbs, the rest of the olive oil, the lemon juice, beetroot and the tomatoes, and stir to combine.

Season with salt and pepper, then divide between 2 lunch boxes.

Preparation time 10 minutes,
plus cooling
Cooking time 40 minutes

The key to this salad is the onion being very finely sliced; its sweetness, combined with the carrots, really makes this dish.

Roasted carrots, chickpeas, pomegranate, cumin & yogurt

3 carrots, peeled and halved lengthways

1 onion, finely sliced

1 tablespoon cumin seeds

1 sprig of rosemary

100ml (3½fl oz) olive oil

400g (14oz) can of chickpeas, drained and rinsed

a few sprigs of dill, leaves and stems finely chopped

a few sprigs of coriander, leaves and stems finely chopped

2 tablespoons Greek yogurt

seeds of 1 pomegranate

sea salt flakes and freshly ground black pepper

Preheat the oven to 180°C fan (400°F), Gas Mark 6.

Put the carrots, onion, cumin seeds, rosemary and olive oil in a roasting tray, and season with salt and pepper. Give the ingredients a good mix, then cover with foil and roast for 30 minutes.

Remove the tray from the oven, lift off the foil and stir in the chickpeas. Then pop the foil back on and roast for a further 10 minutes.

Remove from the oven and let the vegetable mixture cool, then add the dill and coriander.

Divide the salad between 2 lunch boxes, and finish by topping each with a tablespoon of yogurt and half the pomegranate seeds. Serve cold.

MAKES 2

Preparation time 20 minutes,
plus cooling
Cooking time 25 minutes

I first ate this for lunch in Miami in a Japanese restaurant and thought it was a brilliant idea. You can add literally anything you like and it's fresh, healthy, light and – most importantly – tasty! You can find ready-made Japanese pickles in Asian food stores or larger supermarkets.

Japanese chirashi bowl with whatever you fancy

160g (5¾oz) sushi rice

210ml (7½fl oz) water

75ml (5 tablespoons) rice vinegar

1 tablespoon white sesame seeds, toasted

1 tablespoon black sesame seeds, toasted

TO FINISH
(OR ANYTHING ELSE YOU FANCY)

sunflower oil, for cooking

4–5 shiitake mushrooms, finely sliced

2 tablespoons soy sauce

100g (3½oz) fresh raw tuna loin, cut into 5mm (¼-inch) cubes

100g (3½oz) fresh raw skinless salmon fillet, cut into 5mm (¼-inch) cubes

3 spring onions, finely sliced

TO SERVE

2 teaspoons Japanese pickled ginger

2 teaspoons Japanese pickled cucumber

2 teaspoons Japanese pickled radish

a few sprigs of coriander, leaves roughly chopped

First, prepare your rice. Put the rice into a sieve and wash thoroughly in cold water, changing the water constantly until it is clear rather than cloudy.

Next, add the water to a saucepan with the rice. I learned from Tim Anderson, the incredibly talented chef, that to cook Japanese rice you should add 1.3 times the amount of water to rice, by weight, and it works every time. Since 208ml would be the exact amount for this recipe and is pretty precise, I think 210ml will be fine!

Place the pan over a high heat and bring to the boil. Reduce the heat to as low as possible and put a lid on. Cook for 15 minutes, without lifting the lid at all.

After 15 minutes, turn off the heat and remove the lid. Fluff the rice up with a fork, then let it sit at room temperature with the lid half on until it's cooled.

Heat a splash of oil in a nonstick frying pan and sauté the shiitake mushrooms over a medium heat for about 10 minutes until cooked and browned.

Add the soy sauce and reduce so that the mushrooms soak it all up, then remove from the heat and let them cool.

To make up the lunch boxes, first season the rice with the vinegar and sesame seeds. Divide between 2 boxes and top with the tuna, salmon, shiitake, spring onions, pickles and coriander, shared between them. When ready to eat, stir all the elements together and enjoy.

Preparation time 10 minutes,
plus cooling
Cooking time 25 minutes

Once I'd had my first frittata, I was hooked. They are really versatile, and perfect for lunches and picnics as they are so easy to transport.

Courgette & pea frittata with feta cheese

olive oil, for cooking

1 onion, finely chopped

1 courgette, cut into 5mm (¼-inch) cubes

2 handfuls of frozen peas (or fresh if in season), defrosted

4 eggs

100g (3½oz) feta cheese, crumbled

a few sprigs of mint, leaves finely chopped

sea salt flakes and freshly ground black pepper

Heat a splash of olive oil in a small nonstick frying pan about 16cm (6¼-inches) in diameter and sweat the onion for 5–6 minutes over a medium heat without colouring. Season with a pinch of salt.

Next, add the courgette and sweat for about 8 minutes until soft, covering the pan with a lid after the first few minutes. Add the peas and stir until hot.

Crack the eggs into a mixing bowl, beat together and season with salt and pepper.

Reduce the heat under the pan, then add the eggs to the peas and courgette along with the feta and stir quickly, until everything is evenly distributed.

Turn on your grill to a medium heat.

Meanwhile, let the egg mixture sizzle on the hob for 8–10 minutes until all the ingredients are cooked through. The centre of the frittata will still be a little soft, so place under the grill to finish cooking for 1 minute.

Carefully turn the frittata out on to a plate and let it cool a little before either eating warm then and there or cooling in the refrigerator ready for lunch.

Preparation time 10 minutes
Cooking time none

Fresh and zingy, this is a perfect summer salad. "Hot smoking" means the fish has been smoked at a higher temperature, which has also cooked it, so it can be flaked.

Smoked trout, pearl barley & mojo verde

200g (7oz) cooked, ready-to-eat pearl barley

150g (5½oz) skinless hot-smoked rainbow trout

sea salt flakes and freshly ground black pepper

MOJO VERDE

4 garlic cloves, peeled

large handful of coriander leaves

½ teaspoon cumin seeds, toasted

pinch of sea salt flakes

juice of 2 limes

about 100ml (3½fl oz) olive oil, for binding

First, make the mojo verde. Blend all the ingredients together in a blender, gradually adding enough olive oil while the blender is running until you have a pesto-like consistency. Cover and store in the refrigerator until needed for up to 2 days.

Put the cooked pearl barley and 2 tablespoons of the mojo verde in a mixing bowl and mix well.

Flake in the smoked trout, then fold into the barley mixture. Season with salt and pepper.

Divide between 2 lunch boxes and store in the refrigerator until ready to eat.

Preparation time 10 minutes
Cooking time 20 minutes

Slightly spicy and packed full of flavour, this is one of my go-to summer salads for a portable lunch and it also works really well for a barbecue, too.

Harissa couscous salad

100g (3½oz) butternut squash, peeled, deseeded and cut into 2cm (¾-inch) dice

75ml (5 tablespoons) olive oil

200g (7oz) couscous

2 tablespoons harissa paste

10 cherry tomatoes, quartered

a few sprigs of mint, leaves finely chopped

a few sprigs of coriander, leaves and stems finely chopped

80g (2¾oz) firm goats' cheese, cut into 1cm (½-inch) dice

juice of 1 lemon

sea salt flakes and freshly ground black pepper

Preheat the oven to 180°C fan (400°F), Gas Mark 6.

Put the squash in a roasting tray and toss with half the olive oil, season with salt and pepper and roast for 20 minutes until cooked.

Remove from the oven and let it cool.

Meanwhile, cook the couscous according to the packet instructions, then let it cool.

Mix the harissa paste with the rest of the olive oil.

Add the couscous, roasted squash, cherry tomatoes, mint, coriander, goats' cheese, lemon juice and the harissa mixture to a large mixing bowl and fold together. Check the seasoning.

Divide between 2 lunch boxes and store in the refrigerator until ready to eat.

Preparation time 15 minutes,
plus soaking and cooling
Cooking time 35 minutes

A good winter warmer, curried lentil soup – a bit like dhal – has miraculous healing powers when you're feeling a little down in the colder months. A perfect pick-me-up.

Curried lentil soup

1 onion, roughly chopped

40g (1½oz) fresh root ginger, peeled

2 garlic cloves

1 red chilli

1 tablespoon ground cumin

1 tablespoon ground coriander

1 tablespoon Madras curry powder

1 teaspoon ground turmeric

vegetable oil, for cooking

400g (14oz) can of chopped tomatoes

150g (5½oz) dried Puy lentils, soaked in cold water overnight, then drained

500ml (18fl oz) chicken or vegetable stock

1 large sprig of coriander, finely chopped

sea salt flakes and freshly ground black pepper

4 tablespoons Greek yogurt, to serve

Blend the onion, ginger, garlic and chilli together in a blender until you have a smooth purée.

Heat a flameproof casserole dish over a medium heat and toast the ground cumin and coriander, curry powder and turmeric for 1 minute until you can smell the gorgeous aromas.

Next, add a splash of vegetable oil and the puréed onion mixture. Season with salt and sauté together for 3–4 minutes.

Stir in the chopped tomatoes, drained lentils and stock and bring to the boil. Then reduce the heat, pop the lid on and simmer for 30 minutes until the lentils are cooked.

Add the chopped coriander and turn off the heat. Check the seasoning and let the soup cool before storing in the refrigerator until needed. Reheat the soup to serve, stirring in 1 tablespoon of Greek yogurt per person just before serving.

Preparation time 10 minutes,
plus cooling
Cooking time 30 minutes

Another warming lunch recipe that's perfect for winter. Try adding some smoked bacon or chorizo to the onions for an extra hit of flavour.

Quinoa & black bean chowder with spiced avocado & soured cream

olive oil, for cooking

2 onions, finely chopped

2 carrots, peeled and cut into 1cm (½-inch) dice

2 garlic cloves, finely chopped

pinch of chilli flakes

1 tablespoon tomato purée

500ml (18fl oz) vegetable stock

100g (3½oz) cooked, ready-to-eat quinoa

100g (3½oz) drained, canned black beans

sea salt flakes and freshly ground black pepper

2 tablespoons soured cream, to serve

SPICED AVOCADO

1 avocado, peeled and stoned

juice of 1 lime,

a few sprigs of coriander, leaves and stems finely chopped

1 small red chilli, finely chopped

sea salt flakes and freshly ground black pepper

Pour a splash of olive oil in a large saucepan over a medium heat and sweat the onions, carrots, garlic and chilli flakes for 8–10 minutes until softened.

Season with salt and pepper, add the tomato purée and cook for 3–4 minutes.

Pour in the stock and bring to the boil, then stir in the cooked quinoa and black beans. Simmer for 15 minutes over a low heat.

Meanwhile, mix all the ingredients for the spiced avocado together and season with salt and pepper. Cover and refrigerate.

Once the 15 minutes has passed, turn off the heat and let the chowder cool before storing in the refrigerator.

Reheat the chowder before serving, and add a good spoonful each of the spiced avocado and the soured cream, then stir in to enrich the chowder and bring it all together.

SERVES 2–3

Preparation time 10 minutes,
plus cooling
Cooking time 30 minutes

This is based on the Roman dish *vignole* and makes an incredibly nourishing lunch. I definitely recommend a slice or two of buttered sourdough alongside.

Italian spring vegetable stew with smoked pancetta & soft-boiled egg

80g (2¾oz) butter

1 onion, finely chopped

2 garlic cloves, finely chopped

160g (5¾oz) smoked pancetta lardons

1 sprig of rosemary

1 sprig of thyme

1 bay leaf

2 leeks, trimmed, cleaned and cut into rounds 1cm (½-inch) thick

1 glass of white wine

500ml (18fl oz) chicken stock

handful of frozen peas

handful of runner beans, trimmed and cut into 1cm (½-inch) pieces

10 asparagus spears, woody ends removed, cut into 1cm (½-inch) pieces

200g (7oz) baby spinach, washed

1 large sprig of mint, finely chopped

sea salt flakes and freshly ground black pepper

1 egg per person, cooked in boiling water for 6 minutes and refreshed in iced water, to serve

Melt the butter in a flameproof casserole dish over a medium heat and sweat the onion and garlic with the pancetta, rosemary, thyme and bay leaf for 12 minutes. You want the fat to come out of the pancetta and the onion to be softened.

Next, add the leeks, season with salt and pepper and put the lid on, then continue to sweat for another 6 minutes.

Add the white wine and reduce by three-quarters.

Pour in the stock and bring to the boil, then add the peas, runner beans and asparagus. Bring back to the boil, then reduce the heat and simmer for 5–6 minutes.

Remove the rosemary, thyme and bay leaf, then stir in the baby spinach and mint and check the seasoning.

Remove from the heat and let the stew cool before storing in the refrigerator.

Reheat before serving and divide between bowls. Top each with a soft-boiled egg, shelled, cut in half and seasoned with salt and pepper.

Preparation time 10 minutes,
plus cooling
Cooking time 1 hour

Jerk flavours are so interesting and you can buy some great-quality shop-bought marinades. This recipe would be ideal if you have any leftover chicken from a roast; just use the jerk paste on the potatoes instead.

Jerk chicken with sweet potato & corn

2 sweet potatoes, peeled and diced into 2cm (¾-inch) pieces

vegetable oil

2 tablespoons jerk seasoning paste

4 chicken legs

2 x 198g (7oz) cans of sweetcorn kernels, drained

3 spring onions, finely sliced

about 10g (¼ oz) coriander, leaves and stems finely chopped

sea salt flakes and freshly ground black pepper

Preheat the oven to 180°C fan (400°F), Gas Mark 6.

Put the sweet potatoes in a roasting tray and toss in a little vegetable oil. Season with salt and pepper.

Massage the jerk paste into the chicken legs in a mixing bowl and place in among the sweet potato.

Roast for 55 minutes or until the chicken is cooked through and nicely browned.

Remove from the oven and transfer the chicken to a plate to cool.

Add the sweetcorn and spring onions to the tray with the sweet potato and stir in. Pop back in the oven for 5 more minutes.

Remove from the oven and let the vegetables cool.

Flake the chicken into the tray of sweet potatoes, discarding the bones. Add the coriander and stir everything together. Store in the refrigerator until ready to reheat and serve.

Starters, nibbles & snacks

Dips

For these recipes, you'll need to use a food processor or a blender.
I prefer to use a NutriBullet at home as it's small, has fewer parts
and is easier to clean.

I've included a couple of recipes for "scoopers", but equally,
if strapped for time, simple grilled ciabatta or even
a packet of crisps will do the job.

SEASONAL CRUDITÉS – WHAT TO EAT & WHEN

Crispbreads, cheesy pastries, crisps and bruschetta all make great vehicles for the tasty dips in this section, but there are also wonderful vegetables that fit the purpose just as well.

Vegetables, especially raw, are an easy way of ensuring plenty of nourishment and, most importantly, if you buy good-quality ones at the right time of year, you're on to a winner.

I can't emphasize enough how important it is to get them from your local greengrocer or farmers' market – the difference in quality is as night is to day and you'll really appreciate it. Plus, the produce looks great on the dinner table.

Here's a seasonal guide to some of my favourites that I like to eat throughout the year.

SPRING	SUMMER	AUTUMN	WINTER
asparagus **C/R**	beetroot **C**	beetroot **C**	beetroot **C**
Little Gem lettuce **R**	broccoli **C**	celery **R**	cauliflower **R**
new potatoes, such as	carrots **R**	kohlrabi **R**	celery **R**
Jersey Royals **C**	celery **R**	Little Gem lettuce **R**	chicory **R**
radicchio **R**	cherry tomatoes **R**	radicchio **R**	Little Gem lettuce **R**
	courgette flowers **R**		Purple sprouting
	courgettes **R**		broccoli **C**
	fennel **R**		radicchio **R**
	Little Gem lettuce **R**		
	peppers **R**		
	radicchio **R**		
	radish **R**		

C = cooked
R = raw

SERVES 4

Preparation time 10 minutes
Cooking time 50 minutes

Aubergines are brilliant carriers of flavour and are a great match with harissa. This dip has some of the aubergine left chunky to give a nice texture.

Harissa & aubergine

2 aubergines
olive oil, for cooking
1 garlic clove, finely sliced
2 tablespoons harissa paste
a few sprigs of mint, leaves picked and finely sliced
sea salt flakes and freshly ground black pepper

Preheat the oven to 160°C fan (350°F), Gas Mark 4.

Cut the aubergines in half lengthways, then score the flesh in a crisscross pattern. Place them cut sides up in a roasting tray and drizzle with olive oil. Scatter the garlic slices on top and season with salt and pepper.

Roast for 40 minutes until the flesh is soft.

When cooked, remove the aubergines from the oven and scoop out the flesh into a mixing bowl. You may want to run a knife over the flesh to break it down a little. Add the harissa and mix together.

Pop the aubergine mixture into a nonstick frying pan over a medium heat and cook down for 6–7 minutes. Check the seasoning.

At this stage, either serve it chunky or blend it if you prefer a smoother dip. Serve in a bowl with the mint scattered on top.

SERVES 4

Preparation time 10 minutes
Cooking time 15 minutes

This cheesy spinach dip brings back memories of my first visit to America. Artichoke dip was very popular in lots of the restaurants I went to and it's very similar to this. It's all about the cheese!

Cheesy spinach dip

1kg (2lb 4oz) spinach leaves, washed and stems removed
2 tablespoons crème fraîche
whole nutmeg, for grating
50g (1¾oz) mature Cheddar cheese, grated
sea salt flakes and freshly ground black pepper

Blanch the spinach in a pan of salted boiling water for 1 minute. Drain, refresh in iced water, then dry really well in a clean tea towel until you've got rid of as much water as possible.

Roughly chop the spinach, then add to your food processor along with the crème fraîche and blend until almost smooth.

Transfer the spinach mixture to a saucepan. Add a grating of nutmeg and season with salt and plenty of black pepper.

When ready to serve, put the pan over a low heat, add the Cheddar and gently bring to the boil. The cheese will start to bring it all together while getting lovely and melty. Serve in a warmed bowl straight away.

SERVES 4–6

Preparation time 10 minutes, plus resting
Cooking time 25 minutes

These crispbreads are my favourite to go with a dip. If you have a pasta machine, it will make rolling the dough even easier.

Olive oil crispbread scoopers

250g (9oz) plain flour
3 tablespoons olive oil, plus extra for oiling and brushing
120ml (4fl oz) water
1 teaspoon baking powder
pinch of sea salt flakes

Add all the ingredients to the bowl of a stand mixer fitted with the dough hook and knead on a medium speed for 5 minutes until the dough is smooth. Transfer to a bowl, cover with clingfilm and refrigerate for 1 hour to rest.

Preheat an oven to 180°C fan (400°F), Gas Mark 6. Line a baking sheet with baking paper.

On a lightly oiled work surface, roll out the dough into a square sheet as thinly as possible.

Using a fork, prick over the whole sheet making lots of tiny holes.

Cut into roughly 5cm (2-inch) squares and transfer to the lined baking sheet. Brush each square with a little olive oil, then bake for 25 minutes until golden brown and crisp.

Remove the crispbreads from the oven and let them cool completely on the baking sheet.

SERVES 4

Preparation time 5 minutes
Cooking time 10 minutes

This is based on the wonderful romesco sauce from Spain. It's so summery and a staple in my refrigerator at home.

Roasted pepper & almond dip

4 tablespoons olive oil
1 slice of bread, preferably sourdough
50g (1¾oz) flaked almonds
2 garlic cloves, crushed
50ml (2fl oz) sherry vinegar
100g (3½oz) roasted red peppers from a jar
sea salt flakes and freshly ground black pepper

Heat a nonstick frying pan over a medium heat. Pour in half the olive oil and colour the bread on both sides until dark brown. Transfer from the pan to a food processor.

Add the rest of the oil to the same pan, then add the almonds with the garlic and colour these, too, until nicely browned. Transfer to the food processor along with the oil in the pan.

Add the sherry vinegar, a pinch of salt and pepper and the roasted peppers and blend all the ingredients together until smooth.

Clockwise from top left: Harissa & aubergine; Olive oil crispbread scoopers; Roasted pepper & almond dip, Cheesy spinach dip.

Preparation time 5 minutes
Cooking time 1 minute

This is a nice alternative to the pesto we all know and love. It has a deeper, earthier flavour, which I really like. It also works well spooned on to stews at the end before serving, and on winter broths, too.

Parsley, garlic & walnut pesto

2 garlic cloves, peeled
large handful of flat leaf parsley
30g (1oz) Parmesan cheese, finely grated
5 walnuts
about 100ml (3½fl oz) olive oil
sea salt flakes and freshly ground black pepper

Bring a pan of salted water to the boil. Add the garlic cloves, then 30 seconds later add the parsley. After 10 seconds, strain and refresh the garlic and parsley in iced water.

Put the blanched garlic and parsley in a blender along with the Parmesan and the walnuts. Blend all the ingredients together, gradually adding enough olive oil while the blender is running until you have a thick pesto consistency. Season with salt and pepper before serving.

Preparation time 15 minutes, plus cooling
Cooking time 25 minutes

This dip also works well using pumpkin, or even carrot.

Butternut squash & feta dip

100g (3½oz) butternut squash, peeled, deseeded and chopped into 2–3cm (¾–1¼-inch) chunks
2 garlic cloves (unpeeled), bashed
pinch of chilli flakes
a sprig of rosemary
50ml (2fl oz) olive oil, plus extra for drizzling
50g (1¾oz) feta cheese, crumbled into small pieces
pinch of za'atar
sea salt flakes and freshly ground black pepper

Preheat an oven to 180°C (400°F) Gas Mark 6.

Put the butternut squash, garlic cloves, chilli flakes, rosemary and olive oil in a roasting tin. Season with salt and pepper and give it all a good mix.

Roast for 25 minutes until the squash is cooked and just starting to get some colour.

Remove from the oven and, when cool enough to handle, discard the rosemary and the skins of the garlic, then let it all cool completely.

Add to a food processor and pulse to coarsely blend – the texture should be slightly chunky. Season with salt and pepper.

Stir in the feta and serve with a drizzle of extra olive oil over the top and a sprinkle of za'atar.

SERVES 4

Preparation time 10 minutes
Cooking time 1 minute

I first started making this at a supper club I was doing a few years ago and it was an instant hit. It's fresh and healthy and, if you take out the yogurt, it's vegan, too.

Pea hummus with avocado & lime

100g (3½oz) frozen peas
1 avocado, peeled, stoned and roughly chopped
finely grated zest and juice of 2 limes
2 tablespoons Greek yogurt
a few sprigs of mint, leaves picked
a few sprigs of coriander
50ml (2fl oz) olive oil, plus extra for drizzling
sea salt flakes and freshly ground black pepper

Blanch the peas in a pan of salted boiling water for 1 minute, then drain and refresh in iced water.

Drain again and put in a food processor or blender along with all the other ingredients, then blitz until almost smooth. Season with salt and pepper.

To serve, drizzle a little olive oil over the top and finish with some salt flakes.

SERVES 4

Preparation time 5 minutes
Cooking time none

Do cook raw beetroot for this recipe if you prefer – boil them whole until tender or roast in the oven wrapped in foil. A splash of sherry vinegar at the end will give them the acidity of pickled beetroot.

Beetroot & tahini

250g (9oz) drained pickled beetroot
40g (1½oz) tahini
50ml (2fl oz) olive oil, plus extra for drizzling
pinch each of black and white sesame seeds, toasted
sea salt flakes and freshly ground black pepper

Put the pickled beetroot and tahini paste in a food processor, along with the olive oil, and blend until almost smooth. Season with salt and pepper.

To serve, drizzle over a little extra olive oil and sprinkle over the sesame seeds.

SERVES 4–6

Preparation time 15 minutes,
plus resting
Cooking time 20 minutes

Inspired by the cheesy crackers I loved when I was growing up, these make a great alternative to crispbreads. The cheese adds a lovely savouriness that works really well with all the dips.

Cheesy biscuit scoopers

100g (3½oz) plain flour, plus extra for dusting

50g (1¾oz) unsalted butter, softened

200g (7oz) mature Cheddar cheese, grated

pinch of sea salt flakes

1 teaspoon smoked paprika

Put all the ingredients in a food processor and blitz together to form a dough. Wrap the dough in clingfilm and let it rest in the refrigerator for 1 hour.

Preheat the oven to 170°C fan (375°F), Gas Mark 5. Line a baking sheet with baking parchment.

Roll out the dough on a lightly floured work surface until 2mm (1/16-inch) thick. Using a 4cm (1½-inch) cutter, cut into rounds and transfer to the lined baking sheet.

Prick each round a few times with a fork, then bake for 20 minutes until golden brown and crisp.

Remove the biscuits from the oven and let them cool completely on the baking sheet.

SERVES 4

Preparation time 5 minutes
Cooking time 5 minutes

I fell in love with this Middle Eastern pesto a few years ago and can't stop eating it now. It tastes much better than the stuff you can buy in the shops and it gives any dish a massive flavour boost. Try adding a spoonful over some slow-cooked lamb just before serving.

Zhoug

1 tablespoon cumin seeds

1 tablespoon coriander seeds

large handful of coriander

finely grated zest and juice of 1 lime

1 green chilli, roughly chopped

1 garlic clove, peeled

pinch of sugar

about 100ml (3½fl oz) olive oil

sea salt flakes and freshly ground black pepper

Toast the cumin and coriander seeds in a dry frying pan over a low heat for 4–5 minutes, taking care not to burn, then let them cool.

Put in a blender along with all the other ingredients and blitz together until you have a pesto-like consistency. Season with salt and pepper before serving.

Preparation time 10 minutes
Cooking time 10 minutes

The flavour from griddling the asparagus combined with the zingy buttermilk makes for a lovely contrast.

Asparagus with buttermilk & roasted almonds

150ml (¼ pint) buttermilk

finely grated zest and juice of 1 lemon

2 tablespoons olive oil

20 asparagus spears, woody ends removed

handful of roasted salted Spanish almonds

pinch of smoked paprika

handful of watercress leaves

sea salt flakes and freshly ground black pepper

Heat a griddle pan over a medium heat.

Meanwhile, mix the buttermilk and lemon juice together in a mixing bowl and season with salt and pepper.

Drizzle half the olive oil over the asparagus and season with salt and pepper. Griddle, in batches, turning every couple of minutes for 6–7 minutes until char marks appear – the asparagus should be tender but still keeping a little bite.

While the asparagus is cooking, roughly chop the almonds and toss with the paprika.

Dress the watercress with the rest of the olive oil and a pinch of salt.

To serve, divide the grilled asparagus between 4 plates, then dress each one with 3 tablespoons of the buttermilk dressing. Top with some of the watercress, scatter over the almonds and finish with the lemon zest.

SERVES 4

Preparation time 15 minutes
Cooking time 1 hour

There's nothing more comforting and warming than a bowl of good soup and this is one recipe I find myself returning to time and time again. Celeriac works really well here, too.

Parsnip soup with garlic butter mushrooms & chives

4 parsnips, peeled and cut into rounds 1cm (½-inch) thick

50ml (2fl oz) olive oil

1 onion, finely chopped

1 garlic clove, crushed

1 sprig of thyme

1 sprig of rosemary

1 bay leaf

200ml (7fl oz) apple juice or cider

500ml (18fl oz) chicken or vegetable stock

4 tablespoons double cream

sea salt flakes and freshly ground black pepper

finely chopped chives, to garnish

GARLIC BUTTER MUSHROOMS

25g (1oz) butter

3 garlic cloves, peeled

good handful of wild mushrooms, the best you can find – girolles, chanterelles and ceps are all great

Preheat the oven to 180°C fan (400°F), Gas Mark 6.

Put the parsnips in a roasting tray and toss with half the olive oil. Season with salt and pepper and roast for 20 minutes until they get some colour.

Meanwhile, heat a saucepan over a medium heat and pour in the remaining oil. Sauté the onion with the garlic, thyme, rosemary and bay leaf for 10–12 minutes until softened but not coloured. Season with salt and pepper.

Next, add the roasted parsnips to the onion mixture and give it all a good stir. Then add the apple juice or cider, bring to the boil and reduce by three-quarters.

Pour in the chicken stock and bring to the boil, then reduce the heat and simmer for 15 minutes. Stir in the cream and cook for a few more minutes before turning off the heat. Remove the rosemary, thyme and bay leaf, then pour the soup into a blender. Blend until smooth and check the seasoning one more time.

Set aside until gearing up to serve, or let it cool and store in the refrigerator until later.

To serve, start to bring the soup back to the boil. While this is happening, make the garlic butter mushrooms. Heat a nonstick frying pan over a medium heat and add the butter and the garlic. Let the garlic cook gently, taking care not to burn it, for 4–5 minutes.

Once the garlic starts to turn brown, take it out and add the mushrooms. Increase the heat and sauté for 4–5 minutes. Season with salt and pepper at the end.

Serve the soup in warmed bowls with the garlic butter mushrooms sprinkled over, a good pinch of chopped chives and more pepper.

Preparation time 20 minutes,
plus cooling and chilling
Cooking time 25 minutes

There are so few ingredients in these fritters and yet they are so tasty – a firm favourite in my house!

Cheesy polenta fritters

400ml (14fl oz) milk

100g (3½oz) polenta

150g (5½oz) Parmesan cheese, finely grated

50g (1¾oz) plain flour

1 egg, beaten

50g (1¾oz) panko breadcrumbs

sea salt flakes and freshly ground black pepper

vegetable oil, for deep-frying

Heat the milk in a saucepan over a medium heat to just about boiling point, then add the polenta and cook according to the packet instructions – usually about 8 minutes. Season with salt and pepper, then add half the Parmesan.

Cover the pan with a piece of baking paper to prevent a crust forming and let the polenta cool enough to handle.

Stir in the rest of the Parmesan, then roll the polenta mixture into balls about 2.5cm (1-inch) in diameter and chill in the refrigerator for about 1 hour to firm up.

Put the flour, beaten egg and breadcrumbs in 3 separate bowls. Coat each ball firstly in the flour, then the egg and finally the breadcrumbs.

Pour enough vegetable oil into a small saucepan to come 5cm (2-inches) up the sides and heat to 170°C (340°F) – if you don't have a jam thermometer, test if the oil is hot enough by carefully dropping a cube of bread into the oil and, if it sizzles immediately, the oil is ready.

Carefully fry the fritters, in 4 batches, for about 4 minutes until golden brown. Remove with a slotted spoon straight on to kitchen paper to drain the excess oil and keep warm while you cook the remaining batches.

Season with salt and serve hot.

The recipe makes a little extra peperonata, which is no bad thing – it's great stuff to have knocking about.

Peperonata bruschetta with ricotta

PEPERONATA

50ml (2fl oz) olive oil

3 red peppers, cored, deseeded and sliced 5mm (¼-inch) thick

1 red onion, finely sliced

1 garlic clove, finely chopped

5 plum tomatoes, cut into quarters, deseeded and sliced

1 bay leaf

1 sprig of thyme

1 tablespoon demerara sugar

50ml (2fl oz) red wine vinegar

finely grated zest of 1 lemon

sea salt flakes and freshly ground black pepper

BRUSCHETTA

50ml (2fl oz) olive oil

4 slices of sourdough bread

150g (5½oz) ricotta cheese

10 basil leaves, finely chopped

To make the peperonata, heat the olive oil in a large frying pan and gently cook the peppers, onion and garlic for 15–20 minutes without colouring. Season with salt and pepper.

Add the rest of the ingredients and continue to cook for about 45 minutes until the mixture turns to a nice semi-thick sauce consistency. Keep an eye on it and stir often so that it doesn't burn. At the end, remove the bay leaf and thyme before storing. Store in a sterilized jar in the refrigerator until you need it.

When ready to serve, heat a griddle pan over a medium heat. Drizzle the olive oil over the bread and griddle for about 4 minutes on each side until nice and brown.

Transfer the bread to plates and top each slice with a good spoon of the peperonata. Spoon over the ricotta, sprinkle over the chopped basil leaves and season with pepper before serving.

MAKES 8

Preparation time 20 minutes
Cooking time 15 minutes

This classic dish is taken to the next level by breadcrumbing and frying the egg whites, which adds a wonderful crunch.

Crispy devilled eggs

4 eggs

1 tablespoon mayonnaise

1 teaspoon sriracha, or any hot sauce you have

1 sprig of coriander, finely chopped

1 shallot, finely chopped

50g (1¾oz) plain flour

1 egg, beaten

50g (1¾oz) panko breadcrumbs

vegetable oil, for deep-frying

sea salt flakes and freshly ground black pepper

Cook the eggs in a pan of boiling water for 7 minutes. Then drain and cool in iced water.

Shell and halve the boiled eggs, then carefully slide out the yolks, setting the egg whites aside until later. Put them in a blender, add the mayonnaise and sriracha and blend until smooth.

Transfer the yolk mixture to a mixing bowl, add the coriander and shallot and stir through. Season with salt and pepper and set aside.

Put the flour, beaten egg and breadcrumbs into 3 separate bowls. Coat each egg white firstly in the flour, then the egg and finally the breadcrumbs.

Pour enough vegetable oil into a small saucepan to come 5cm (2-inches) up the sides and heat to 170°C (340°F) – if you don't have a jam thermometer, test if the oil is hot enough by carefully dropping a cube of bread into the oil and, if it sizzles immediately, the oil is ready.

Carefully fry the egg whites, in 2 batches, for about 4 minutes until golden brown. Remove with a slotted spoon straight on to kitchen paper to drain the excess oil. Season with salt.

Spoon the yolk mixture into the egg white cavities. Arrange on a serving plate and serve warm.

SERVES 4

Preparation time 10 minutes
Cooking time 1 hour

A great sharing starter for a Mexican-inspired feast. I've always loved nachos – the crispy chips with plenty of cheese are wonderful. I've used sweet potato here rather than a meat-based ragout which I think works really well.

Sweet potato chilli nachos

olive oil, for cooking

1 onion, finely chopped

2 garlic cloves, finely chopped

1 teaspoon cumin seeds

1 tablespoon smoked paprika

pinch of chilli flakes

1 tablespoon tomato purée

4 sweet potatoes, peeled and cut into 1cm (½-inch) cubes

400g (14oz) can of black beans, drained

400g (14oz) can of chopped tomatoes

400ml (14fl oz) vegetable stock

large handful of coriander, chopped

1 large bag of tortilla chips

100g (3½oz) mature Cheddar cheese, grated

2 tablespoons soured cream

sea salt flakes and freshly ground black pepper

Pour a splash of olive oil in a large frying pan over a medium heat and sweat the onion and garlic for 5 minutes without colouring. Season with salt and pepper.

Add the cumin, paprika and chilli flakes and cook for another 2–3 minutes, then stir in the tomato purée and cook for 3 minutes.

Next, add the sweet potatoes and mix in well. Then add the black beans, chopped tomatoes and the vegetable stock and season with salt and pepper.

Cover the pan with a lid and cook over a low heat for 40 minutes, stirring every 10 minutes.

When the 40 minutes is up, add half the chopped coriander.

Preheat an oven to 200°C fan (425°F), Gas Mark 7.

Open the bag of tortilla chips and spread half over the base of a deep baking tray. Add half the sweet potato ragout in an even layer, then add half the Cheddar. Repeat with the remaining tortilla chips, ragout and Cheddar.

Bake for 10 minutes until the cheese is melted and colouring.

Finish with the soured cream spooned evenly over and the rest of the coriander sprinkled on top. Eat straight away.

MAKES 12–15

Preparation time 40 minutes,
plus cooling and chilling
Cooking time 25 minutes

A quicker alternative to traditional croquettes with just as much flavour. Falafel-like in texture with a crunchy coating, these are incredibly moreish.

Spiced chickpea croquettes with mint yogurt

olive oil, for cooking

1 red onion, finely chopped

2 garlic cloves, finely chopped

1 teaspoon cumin seeds

1 teaspoon ground turmeric

pinch of chilli powder

400g (14oz) can of chickpeas, drained and rinsed

small handful of flat leaf parsley, finely chopped

50g (1¾oz) plain flour

1 egg, beaten

50g (1¾oz) panko breadcrumbs

vegetable oil, for deep-frying

sea salt flakes and freshly ground black pepper

MINT YOGURT

100g (3½oz) Greek yogurt

a few sprigs of mint, leaves finely chopped

Pour a splash of olive oil in a nonstick frying pan over a medium heat and sweat the onion and garlic for 4–5 minutes until soft but not coloured. Season with salt and pepper.

Add the cumin, turmeric and chilli powder and cook for another 3 minutes, then turn off the heat and let the onion mixture cool.

Blend three-quarters of the chickpeas in a food processor until smooth, then transfer to a mixing bowl. Add the cooked onion mixture and the parsley and mix together well. Check the seasoning.

Roll the chickpea mixture into balls about 2.5cm (1-inch) in diameter and chill in the refrigerator for 2 hours to firm up.

Meanwhile, mix the yogurt and mint together, then refrigerate until ready to serve.

When the chickpea balls have firmed up, put the flour, beaten egg and breadcrumbs in 3 separate bowls. Coat each ball firstly in the flour, then the egg and finally the breadcrumbs.

Pour enough vegetable oil into a small saucepan to come 5cm (2-inches) up the sides and heat to 170°C (340°F) – if you don't have a jam thermometer, test if the oil is hot enough by carefully dropping a cube of bread into the oil and, if it sizzles immediately, the oil is ready.

Carefully fry the croquettes, in 4 batches, for about 4 minutes until golden brown. Remove with a slotted spoon straight on to kitchen paper to drain the excess oil, and keep warm while you cook the remaining batches.

Season with salt and serve hot alongside the mint yogurt for dipping.

MAKES 12

Preparation time 30 minutes,
plus resting
Cooking time 25 minutes

Sausage rolls are a British classic that I love to play around with. As well as making a great starter, these are ideal for a picnic or a snack for a long trip.

Pork & Cheddar sausage rolls

300g (10½oz) Cumberland
sausagemeat

2 tablespoons Marmite

100g (3½oz) mature Cheddar
cheese, grated

2 tablespoons red onion chutney or
tomato Chutney (*see* page 26)

500g (1lb 2oz) block of puff pastry

plain flour, for dusting

1 egg, beaten

1 tablespoon white sesame seeds

sea salt flakes and freshly ground
black pepper

Mix the sausagemeat with the Marmite, Cheddar and red onion chutney in a mixing bowl. Season with salt and pepper.

Cut the pastry block in half. Take one half and roll out on a floured work surface into a rectangle about 30 x 21cm (12 x 8¼-inches), and 5mm (¼-inch) thick. Turn the pastry so that the longer edge is facing you.

Divide the sausagemeat in half. Shape one portion of meat into a long sausage and place across the middle of the pastry sheet. Brush with egg all around the pastry edge (reserve any remaining egg). Roll the pastry over the sausagement and overlap the egg-washed border by a few centimetres. Using a fork, press down and seal the pastry seam well, then place seam side down on a plate. Repeat with the remaining pastry and sausagemeat.

Transfer to the refrigerator to rest for an hour.

Preheat the oven to 180°C fan (400°F), Gas Mark 6. Line a baking sheet with baking parchment.

Remove the sausage rolls from the refrigerator, then cut a diagonal slash every centimetre (½-inch) or so in the top of each roll all the way along. Cut each roll into 6, then transfer the rolls to the lined baking sheet.

Brush each sausage roll generously with egg wash, sprinkle over the sesame seeds, then bake for 25 minutes until golden brown.

Remove the sausage rolls from the oven and let them cool on a wire rack.

This is one of my favourite nibbles to make at home. These are ideal to prepare ahead of time, popping them in the oven as your guests arrive.

Bacon-wrapped dates with chorizo & Cheddar stuffing

100g (3½oz) cooking chorizo, skins removed

25g (1oz) mature Cheddar cheese, grated

25g (1oz) cream cheese

10 dates, stoned

10 smoked streaky bacon rashers

MUSTARD MAYONNAISE

1 tablespoon wholegrain mustard

2 tablespoons mayonnaise

Preheat the oven to 180°C fan (400°F), Gas Mark 6.

Cut the chorizo into 5mm (¼-inch) chunks and put in a mixing bowl. Using a wooden spoon, break them down a little more, then add the Cheddar and cream cheese and mix together well.

Roll into balls, about 15g (½oz) each in weight – you should get 10.

Next, make a cut along the side of each date, without cutting through to the other side. Open out on the work surface, flattening them out as much as possible. You may want to use a rolling pin.

Add a ball of the chorizo mixture to each date and then close up the date. Wrap each stuffed date with a streaky bacon rasher, and use a cocktail stick to hold each together.

Place on a baking sheet and bake for about 20 minutes until the bacon is nicely coloured and the filling is cooked.

Meanwhile, make the mustard mayonnaise by mixing both ingredients together.

Serve the dates hot with the mustard mayonnaise in a small dish on the side.

SERVES 4

Preparation time 25 minutes
Cooking time 40 minutes

A great warming dish that's best eaten with big hunks of bread. Sprinkling some crispy bacon bits on the top would be a great addition, too.

Creamy clam chowder

CLAMS

500g (1lb 2oz) fresh clams, washed in cold water (discard any with broken shells)

1 glass of white wine

1 shallot, finely chopped

1 garlic clove, crushed

1 sprig of thyme

CHOWDER

olive oil, for cooking

1 onion, finely chopped

1 garlic clove, finely chopped

1 sprig of thyme

1 bay leaf

pinch of chilli flakes

200ml (7fl oz) double cream

200ml (7fl oz) chicken stock

2 potatoes, peeled and cut into 1cm (½-inch) dice

a few sprigs of flat leaf parsley, leaves finely chopped

sea salt flakes and freshly ground black pepper

Put the clams, white wine, shallot, garlic and thyme in a mixing bowl. Heat a saucepan over a medium heat and, when hot, tip the contents of the bowl inside and cover with a lid straight away. Cook for 3–4 minutes until the clams open (discard any that remain closed), at which point take the pan off the heat.

Strain the stock through a fine sieve to remove any dirt and grit. Pick the clam meat out of the shells, saving a few in the shell for garnish.

To make the chowder, heat another saucepan over a medium heat, add a splash of olive oil and sweat the onion with the garlic, thyme, bay leaf and chilli flakes for 8–10 minutes until soft but not coloured. Season with salt and pepper.

Next, add the clam stock, bring to the boil and reduce by three-quarters.

Then stir in the cream, chicken stock and diced potatoes, reduce the heat and simmer for about 20 minutes until the potatoes are cooked. Keep an eye that the chowder doesn't catch on the bottom of the pan.

Once the potatoes are cooked, stir in the clams and the chopped parsley, then check the seasoning. Serve in warmed bowls, garnished with the reserved clams in their shells.

MAKES 8

Preparation time 15 minutes
Cooking time none

I love a retro classic, and it doesn't get much better than a prawn cocktail. These are ideal to start a meal or to add to a buffet table, and can be made in advance.

Prawn cocktail lettuce cups

½ avocado
finely grated zest and juice of 1 lime
2 tablespoons mayonnaise
1 teaspoon sriracha hot sauce
200g (7oz) cooked peeled jumbo prawns
1 head of Little Gem lettuce
sea salt flakes and freshly ground black pepper

TO GARNISH
finely chopped chives
paprika

Peel the avocado and remove the stone, then cut into 8 thin slices and put into a mixing bowl. Add the lime zest, reserving some for garnish, and juice and season with salt and pepper. Set aside for later.

In another mixing bowl, mix the mayonnaise and the sriracha hot sauce together.

Dry the prawns well with kitchen paper and cut them in half lengthways. Add to the mayonnaise sauce and mix together well.

Remove and discard the outer leaves from the lettuce. Then peel away 8 leaves for the lettuce cups and wash and dry well. Save the rest of the lettuce for another time.

To assemble, lay out the lettuce leaves on a plate. Add 1 slice of avocado to the bottom of each lettuce leaf, followed by 1 teaspoon of the prawn mixture on top.

To serve, sprinkle with a few chopped chives, a pinch of paprika and a grating of lime zest over each one.

Preparation time 15 minutes,
plus cooling
Cooking time 45 minutes

Making soufflés is great fun and they are really impressive. Savoury ones are much easier to make than sweet ones, so don't be scared to give them a go!

Smoked haddock & Cheddar soufflés

200ml (7fl oz) milk

1 bay leaf

100g (3½oz) smoked haddock, skinned and cut into 2cm (¾-inch) cubes

20g (¾oz) butter, plus a small knob, softened, for brushing the ramekins

20g (¾oz) Parmesan cheese, grated

20g (¾oz) plain flour

80g (2¾oz) mature Cheddar cheese, grated

200ml (7fl oz) double cream

1 tablespoon English mustard

6 eggs, separated

½ small packet (about 5g) of chives, finely chopped

2 handfuls of watercress

sea salt flakes and freshly ground black pepper

MUSTARD DRESSING

2 tablespoons white wine vinegar

1 tablespoon Dijon mustard

4 tablespoons olive oil

Preheat an oven to 180°C fan (400°F), Gas Mark 6.

Put the milk in a saucepan with the bay leaf. Add the smoked haddock and bring to a simmer. As soon as the milk reaches simmering point, turn off the heat and let it cool. Strain the haddock and reserve, keeping the milk, too, but get rid of the bay leaf.

Take 4 x 200ml (7fl oz) ramekins and brush each one with the softened butter. Add the Parmesan and roll the ramekins around so that all the surfaces are coated evenly. Tip out any excess. Set aside until later.

Melt the 20g (¾oz) butter in a saucepan over a medium heat. Add the flour and stir in well. Continue to cook, stirring, for 5–6 minutes until the flour smells a little biscuity. Gradually add the haddock poaching milk while constantly stirring until it's all incorporated and the sauce is smooth.

Add the Cheddar and mix in well, then stir in the cream and the mustard. Check the seasoning. Turn off the heat and let the sauce cool for about 30 minutes. When cooled, stir in the egg yolks and the chives.

Whisk the egg whites in a large mixing bowl with a pinch of salt until stiff. Add one-quarter of the whisked egg whites to the sauce and stir in, then gently fold in the rest in 2 batches, taking care not to knock out any of the air. Finally, gently fold in the cooked smoked haddock.

Spoon the mixture into the prepared ramekins, filling them all the way to the top, then smooth off the surface. Stand the ramekins in a deep ovenproof tray and pour in boiling water from the kettle until it comes up halfway up the sides of the ramekins. Bake for 25 minutes – the tops should be lovely and golden brown.

Meanwhile, whisk all the ingredients for the dressing together and dress the watercress with it.

Carefully remove the soufflés from the oven and serve immediately before they collapse with the watercress salad on the side.

Preparation time 10 minutes
Cooking time 15 minutes

This benefits from having plenty of bread to mop up the juices – arguably the best bit!

Crab claws roasted in garlic butter

8–12 raw, if possible, or cooked crab claws in the shell, 80–100g (2¾–3½oz) each, cracked

100g (3½oz) butter

2 shallots, finely chopped

5 garlic cloves, crushed

2 red chillies, finely sliced into rounds

1 lemon

1 large sprig of flat leaf parsley, chopped

sea salt flakes and freshly ground black pepper

Preheat the oven to 200°C fan (425°F), Gas Mark 7.

If you have fresh crab claws, blanch in salted boiling water for 3 minutes, then drain and let them cool at room temperature. If using cooked crab claws, you can skip this stage.

Put the butter in an ovenproof frying pan over a medium heat, then add the crab claws, shallots, garlic and chillies and give it all a good stir. Season with salt and pepper.

Once the butter starts to bubble, transfer the pan to the oven for 8–10 minutes until heated through and the butter starts to turn brown.

Remove the pan from the oven and carefully lift the claws out on to a plate. Squeeze the juice from the lemon half into the pan while swirling, add the chopped parsley and then pour all over the crab claws.

Preparation time 30 minutes
Cooking time 10 minutes

Tacos have taken the world by storm in recent years even though they've been around forever. There are so many variations, but I especially love these fish versions and they are great with an ice-cold beer or, even better, a Margarita.

Crispy cod tacos with spicy avocado & salsa

1 avocado

1 red onion, finely chopped

1 red chilli, finely chopped

a few sprigs of coriander, finely chopped, plus extra leaves to garnish

finely grated zest and juice of 1 lime

200g (7oz) skinless cod fillet

plain flour, for coating

vegetable oil, for deep-frying

8 small soft corn tortillas, about 10cm (4-inches) in diameter

sea salt flakes and freshly ground black pepper

lime wedges, to serve

TOMATO SALSA

2 plum tomatoes, cut into 1cm (½-inch) pieces

½ red onion (reserved from above)

1 red chilli, finely chopped

a few sprigs of coriander, leaves and stems finely chopped

juice of 1 lime

sea salt flakes and freshly ground black pepper

BATTER

50g (1¾oz) cornflour

50g (1¾oz) plain flour

chilled sparkling water

Peel the avocado, cut in half and remove the stone, then cut into 1cm (½-inch) chunks and put into a mixing bowl. Add half the red onion (reserve the rest for the tomato salsa), the chilli, coriander and lime zest and juice, toss to mix and season with salt and pepper.

Next, make the tomato salsa by mixing all the ingredients together and set aside until later.

To make the batter, combine the flours in a mixing bowl, then whisk in enough chilled sparkling water to make a batter the consistency of single cream. Keep refrigerated while you prepare the cod.

Cut the cod fillet into strips about 2cm (¾-inch) thick, then coat each one in a little flour.

Heat the oil for deep-frying in a deep-fat fryer or a deep saucepan to 170°C (340°F) – if you don't have a jam thermometer, test if the oil is hot enough by carefully dropping a spoonful of batter into the oil and, if it sizzles immediately, the oil is ready. Meanwhile, heat a nonstick frying pan and start to toast the tortillas. When slightly coloured on each side, pop on to a plate while you cook the cod.

Add the floured cod strips to the batter and give them a good mix. Gently lift out piece by piece and carefully add to the hot oil. Cook for about 3 minutes until golden brown, then remove with a slotted spoon straight on to kitchen paper to drain the excess oil. Season with salt and pepper.

To serve, add a spoon of the spicy avocado mixture to each tortilla, then add a spoon of tomato salsa and place a piece of crispy cod on top. Garnish the tacos with the coriander leaves and serve with lime wedges on the side.

Mains

A light and healthy dish that comes to life with the addition of wild garlic pesto. Wild garlic is a brilliant ingredient; fill your boots with it while it's in season because it's soon over.

Grilled cauliflower & broccoli with bulgur wheat salad & wild garlic pesto

olive oil, for cooking

1 teaspoon ground cumin

1 large or 2 small cauliflowers, broken into florets

1 large or 2 small heads of broccoli, broken into florets

2 tablespoons Wild Garlic Pesto (*see* page 125), or to taste

sea salt and freshly ground black pepper

BULGUR WHEAT SALAD

300g (10½oz) cooked, ready-to-eat bulgur wheat

20 cherry tomatoes, halved

a few sprigs of coriander, leaves and stems roughly chopped

a few sprigs of mint, leaves roughly chopped

1 red onion, finely chopped

finely grated zest and juice of 1 lemon

50ml (2fl oz) olive oil

sea salt flakes and freshly ground black pepper

Preheat the oven to 180°C fan (400°F), Gas Mark 6.

Mix all the bulgur wheat salad ingredients together in a mixing bowl and season with salt and pepper.

In another bowl, mix a drizzle of olive oil with the cumin, then toss the cauliflower and broccoli florets in the spiced oil. Season with salt and pepper.

Heat an ovenproof griddle pan over a medium-high heat, add the vegetables and grill for about 3–4 minutes until coloured all over.

Transfer to a roasting tray and bake for 10–12 minutes until the stems are cooked through (check by piercing a thick stem with a knife).

Remove the vegetables from the oven. Serve the salad in bowls with the dressed grilled vegetables on top and the wild garlic pesto on the side for drizzling over.

A hearty, healing chunky soup, perfect for
a cold night's dinner.

Tuscan-style bean soup with parsley & garlic pesto

olive oil, for cooking

200g (7oz) smoked pancetta lardons

2 onions, finely chopped

3 carrots, peeled and cut into 1cm
(½-inch) dice

3 celery sticks, cut into 1cm
(½-inch) dice

4 garlic cloves, finely chopped

1 sprig of rosemary

1 bay leaf

1 tablespoon fennel seeds

pinch of chilli flakes

400g (14oz) can of chopped tomatoes

500ml (18fl oz) chicken stock

400g (14oz) can of cannellini beans,
drained

sea salt flakes and freshly ground
black pepper

PARSLEY & GARLIC PESTO

2 garlic cloves, peeled

large handful of flat leaf parsley

30g (1oz) Parmesan cheese,
finely grated

about 100ml (3½fl oz) olive oil

sea salt flakes and freshly ground
black pepper

To make the pesto, bring a pan of salted water to the boil. Add the garlic, then 30 seconds later add the parsley. After 10 seconds, drain and refresh the garlic and parsley in iced water. Drain well again and pat dry with kitchen paper.

Put the blanched parsley and garlic in a blender along with the Parmesan. Blend the ingredients together, gradually adding enough olive oil while the blender is running until you have a thick pesto consistency. Season with salt and pepper and set aside.

To make the soup, heat a large flameproof casserole dish over a medium heat. Add a splash of olive oil and then the lardons and cook for 3–4 minutes until they start to colour.

Add the onions, carrots, celery, garlic, rosemary, bay leaf, fennel seeds and chilli flakes, season with salt and pepper and sweat for 6–7 minutes without colouring.

Next, pour in the chopped tomatoes and chicken stock and bring to the boil. Then reduce the heat and simmer for 30 minutes.

Stir in the cannellini beans and cook for another 10 minutes. Remove the sprig of rosemary and bay leaf.

Serve in warmed bowls with 1 tablespoon of the pesto on top of each, ready to be stirred in.

Preparation time 20 minutes,
plus standing
Cooking time 1 hour 30 minutes

A delicious Mediterranean-inspired dish that goes great with some peppery rocket and toasted almonds.

Chunky caponata stuffed aubergines

2 aubergines

olive oil, for cooking

2 garlic cloves, finely sliced

1 sprig of thyme, leaves picked

80g (2¾oz) Parmesan cheese

sea salt flakes and freshly ground black pepper

CAPONATA

2 aubergines, cut into 2cm (¾-inch) dice

olive oil, for cooking

1 onion, finely chopped

2 celery sticks, cut into 5mm (¼-inch) dice

2 red peppers, cored, deseeded and cut into 5mm (¼-inch) dice

400g (14oz) tomato passata

100g (3½oz) pitted green olives, roughly chopped

3 tablespoons capers, rinsed

2 tablespoons red wine vinegar

1 teaspoon harissa paste

1½ tablespoons sugar

a few sprigs of flat leaf parsley, leaves roughly chopped

sea salt flakes and freshly ground black pepper

To make the caponata, toss the diced aubergines with a pinch of salt and let them sit in a colander for 30 minutes.

Heat a flameproof casserole dish over a medium heat and add a splash of olive oil. Add the aubergines and cook for 10 minutes until browned. Remove from the pan and set aside to cool.

While the aubergines are cooling, add a little more oil to the same pan and sauté the onion, celery and peppers for 6–7 minutes over a medium heat until soft. Season with salt and pepper, then add the passata and the olives and simmer for 20 minutes.

Next, add the browned aubergines with the capers and stir well, then mix in the vinegar, harissa and sugar and cook for a further 10 minutes.

Remove from the heat and let the caponata cool, then add the chopped parsley. Taste and check the seasoning.

Preheat an oven to 180°C fan (400°F), Gas Mark 6.

Cut each aubergine in half lengthways, then score the flesh in a cross-cross pattern. Add cut sides up to a roasting tray and drizzle with olive oil, then season with salt and pepper. Scatter the garlic and thyme on top.

Roast for 30 minutes or until the flesh is cooked and starting to colour.

Remove from the oven and discard the thyme. Carefully scoop out the aubergine flesh from the skins and add to the caponata, then stir well.

Next, stuff the caponata back inside the aubergine skins and sprinkle the Parmesan on top. Return to the oven for 10 minutes until the cheese is just starting to colour.

SERVES 4

Preparation time 15 minutes,
plus marinating
Cooking time 45 minutes

Middle Eastern flavours are big right now, and rightly so; they are wonderful and fresh. Cooking the chicken on a barbecue takes this dish to another level.

Lebanese-spiced chicken legs with hot hummus & zhoug

4 chicken legs, separated into thighs and drums, scored through the skin about every 1cm (½-inch)

vegetable oil, for cooking

2 handfuls of Tenderstem broccoli

olive oil, for dressing

4 tablespoons Zhoug (*see* page 67)

sea salt flakes

MARINADE

1 teaspoon ground cumin

1 teaspoon ground coriander

pinch of chilli flakes

1 teaspoon fennel seeds

1 teaspoon salt

juice of 1 lemon

4 tablespoons olive oil

sea salt flakes and freshly ground black pepper

HUMMUS

125g (4½oz) canned chickpeas, drained and rinsed

60g (2¼oz) tahini

75ml (5 tablespoons) cold water

juice of 1 lemon

1 garlic clove, peeled

sea salt flakes and freshly ground black pepper

Mix together all the ingredients for the marinade in a mixing bowl, then massage into the chicken legs. If you can, cover and let them marinate for some time in the refrigerator, anything from 1 hour up to 1 day.

Preheat the oven to 170°C fan (375°F), Gas Mark 5.

To make the hummus, add all the ingredients to a blender and blitz until smooth. Season with salt and pepper. Transfer to a saucepan and set aside until ready to dish up.

Heat a cast-iron or other ovenproof frying pan over a medium heat and add a splash of vegetable oil. Add the chicken pieces, skin side down, and colour until nice and brown. Turn over and pop the pan into the oven for 40 minutes.

After 20 minutes, bring a pan of salted water to the boil and blanch the broccoli for 2 minutes. Drain and toss in a little olive oil and salt.

Heat the hummus over a medium heat, taking care not to catch it on the bottom of the pan.

When ready to serve, spoon the hummus on to each plate, then add a few stems of broccoli. Place a thigh and a drum on top, then finish with a good spoon of zhoug on the chicken.

Preparation time 20 minutes
Cooking time 1 hour

I love using a whole chicken this way, so that everyone gets the bit they prefer, but using only legs or breasts is totally fine, too. Even diced cooked chicken works here – just skip the oven steps and add the chicken at the end once the sauce has reduced.

Chicken, potato, leek & mascarpone ragout

vegetable oil, for cooking

1 large chicken, about 2kg (4lb 8oz), separated into thighs, drums and breasts, halved

1 onion, finely chopped

2 leeks, trimmed, cleaned and cut into rounds 5mm (¼-inch) thick

2 garlic cloves, finely chopped

1 bay leaf

4 potatoes, peeled and cut into 2cm (¾-inch) dice

400ml (14fl oz) chicken stock

100ml (3½fl oz) double cream

1 large tablespoon mascarpone cheese

½ bunch (about 15g/½oz) of tarragon, chopped

sea salt flakes and freshly ground black pepper

Preheat an oven to 180°C fan (400°F), Gas Mark 6.

Heat a flameproof casserole dish over a medium heat and add a splash of vegetable oil. Season the chicken with salt and pepper, then seal on both sides until nicely coloured. Remove from the pan to a plate.

Add the onion, leeks, garlic and bay leaf to the same pan (don't clean it first) and season with salt and pepper. Sweat for 8 minutes, taking care not to colour the vegetables too much.

Add the potatoes and stir in, then pour in the stock. Bring to the boil, then return the chicken to the pan, placing it on top, skin side up. Transfer to the oven for 40 minutes until cooked through.

When ready, remove the pan from the oven and again lift the chicken out on to a plate to rest.

Add the cream and mascarpone to the pan, increase the heat, bring to the boil and reduce by half, then stir in the tarragon. Check the seasoning one last time.

Divide the chicken between serving plates and add a good spoon of the sauce on top.

Preparation time 30 minutes,
plus marinating
Cooking time 10 minutes

Grilled lamb and fresh peach is a wonderful
combination; the deep, grilled lamb flavour
contrasts brilliantly with the sweet, juicy fruit.

Herby lamb leg steaks with Israeli couscous & grilled peaches

4 lamb leg steaks, about 180g (6¼oz) each
and 3cm (1¼-inches) thick

MARINADE

a few sprigs of coriander

a few sprigs of mint, leaves picked

a few sprigs of flat leaf parsley

2 jalapeño chillies

5mm (¼-inch) piece of fresh root
ginger, peeled

finely grated zest of ¼ lemon

½ teaspoon ground coriander

½ teaspoon ground cumin

2 cardamom pods

about 50ml (2fl oz) olive oil

sea salt flakes and freshly ground
black pepper

COUSCOUS

4 ripe peaches, stoned and cut
into wedges

300g (10½oz) giant Israeli couscous,
cooked according to the packet
instructions

a few sprigs of mint, leaves picked and
roughly chopped

a few sprigs of flat leaf parsley, roughly
chopped

75ml (5 tablespoons) olive oil

finely grated zest and juice of 1 lemon

sea salt flakes and freshly ground
black pepper

To make the marinade, put all the ingredients in a blender, season well and blitz until smooth.

Pour over the lamb leg steaks in a dish, cover and marinate in the refrigerator for at least 3 hours, preferably overnight.

Light your barbecue, if using, and let the coals burn down until they are glowing white. Otherwise, heat a griddle pan on the hob over a high heat.

To make the couscous, first grill or griddle the peaches until nicely charred on both sides. Do this when the barbecue is at its hottest, so it only takes a minute on each side and stops them getting too soft.

When ready, remove the peaches from the barbecue (or griddle pan) and let them cool. Then add to the couscous along with the other ingredients and mix together. Set aside while you cook the lamb.

Scrape off any excess marinade from the lamb steaks and discard.

Seal the steaks on the barbecue (or griddle pan over a medium-high heat) until nicely coloured on both sides. You want the lamb to be pink in the middle, so ideally cook for 3 minutes on each side. If the barbecue is too hot, move the steaks to the side so they don't burn.

Let them rest for 4–5 minutes before serving with the couscous.

I love food like this, where you can chuck it in the oven and let time make the magic happen. This is an ideal dish for batch cooking and freezing, too.

Slow-cooked Indian spiced lamb shanks with roasted squash mash

4 lamb shanks
vegetable oil, for cooking
2 onions, finely chopped
2 garlic cloves, finely chopped
1 green chilli, finely chopped
1 bay leaf
400g (14oz) can of chopped tomatoes
500ml (18fl oz) chicken stock
large handful of coriander, finely chopped
sea salt flakes and freshly ground black pepper

MARINADE

20g (¾oz) fresh root ginger, peeled
3 garlic cloves, peeled
1 green chilli
seeds from 2 cardamom pods
1 cinnamon stick
1 tablespoon cumin seeds
1 tablespoon coriander seeds
1 tablespoon fennel seeds
1 tablespoon sea salt
1 teaspoon chilli flakes
1 teaspoon ground turmeric
50ml (2fl oz) olive oil

SQUASH MASH

1 large butternut squash
50ml (2fl oz) olive oil
2 garlic cloves (unpeeled), bashed
1 sprig of rosemary
sea salt flakes and freshly ground black pepper

Place all the ingredients for the marinade in a blender and blitz together. Massage into the lamb shanks in a large bowl. If you can, cover with clingfilm and let them marinate in the refrigerator, anything from 1–24 hours.

Preheat an oven to 160°C fan (350°F), Gas Mark 4.

Heat a frying pan over a medium heat and add a splash of vegetable oil. Add the lamb shanks and colour all over until nice and brown.

Meanwhile, heat a large flameproof casserole dish over a medium heat. Add a splash of vegetable oil and sweat the onions, garlic, green chilli and bay leaf for 4–5 minutes without colouring. Season with salt and pepper. Pour in the chopped tomatoes and stock and bring to the boil.

Return the browned lamb shanks to pan and cover the pan with a lid or foil. Transfer to the oven for 3 hours.

After 1½ hours, start preparing the squash mash. Peel the squash, cut in half lengthways and remove the seeds, then cut into 2–3cm (¾–1¼-inch) chunks.

Mix the squash with the olive oil, garlic and rosemary in a mixing bowl, and season with salt and pepper. Transfer to a roasting tray and roast along with the lamb for 1 hour. If the squash starts to colour too much, cover with a sheet of foil.

Remove the squash from the oven and discard the garlic and rosemary. Using a fork, coarsely crush the squash and set aside until ready to serve.

When the lamb shanks are ready (the meat will be falling off the bones), remove from the oven. Carefully lift the shanks out and on to a plate, then cover with foil to keep hot.

Place the pan back on the hob over a high heat and reduce the sauce until it is a thicker consistency, like a pasta sauce.

When the sauce is ready, stir in the coriander. Reheat the squash mash and serve in bowls, with a shank on top and a good ladle of the sauce poured over.

Preparation time 10 minutes
Cooking time 20 minutes

This dish came about from using up some leftover ingredients I had at home. It's quick, cheap and perfect for a warming dinner on the sofa. If strapped for time you can buy the dukkah ready-made; it's a wonderful ingredient to sprinkle over salads, grilled meats and fish.

Harissa beef & cauliflower hash with dukkah

olive oil, for cooking

150g (5½oz) minced beef

1 tablespoon harissa paste

1 onion, finely chopped

2 garlic cloves, finely chopped

1 bay leaf

1 red chilli, finely chopped

1 teaspoon ground cumin

1 cauliflower, broken into 3–4cm (1¼–1½-inch) florets

a few sprigs of coriander, leaves and stems finely chopped

a few sprigs of mint, leaves finely chopped

sea salt flakes and freshly ground black pepper

DUKKAH

50g (1¾oz) blanched hazelnuts

2 tablespoons sesame seeds

1 tablespoon cumin seeds

1 tablespoon coriander seeds

1 tablespoon fennel seeds

pinch of sea salt flakes

To make the dukkah, toast all the ingredients together in a dry frying pan over a low heat for 4–5 minutes, taking care not to burn anything.

Pulse in a blender until you have a course crumb. Once cool, store in an airtight container.

Heat a good splash of olive oil in a large nonstick frying pan over a medium heat. Add the minced beef and, using a wooden spoon, break it down so that it's not too chunky/clumped together. As its starts to colour, add the harissa, onion, garlic, bay leaf, chilli and cumin, and season with salt and pepper.

Continue to cook for 6–7 minutes until the onion becomes softened but not coloured too much (a little colour is OK).

Next, add the cauliflower and a little more oil. Give the pan a good mix, then cover with a lid and cook for a further 5 minutes. The cauliflower should be just cooked.

Finish by stirring in the chopped coriander and mint, then serve in bowls with 1 tablespoon of the dukkah sprinkled on top of each.

Preparation time 25 minutes,
plus cooling
Cooking time 45 minutes

Meatball bakes are so comforting and warming. I serve this with herby couscous to lighten it up a touch from the traditional mashed potatoes or pasta.

Spicy beef meatball bake with herby couscous

olive oil

1 onion, finely chopped

2 garlic cloves, finely chopped

600g (1lb 5oz) minced beef

2 tablespoons harissa paste

4 tablespoons panko breadcrumbs

sea salt flakes and freshly ground black pepper

SAUCE

olive oil

1 onion, finely chopped

2 teaspoons cumin seeds

2 teaspoons ground coriander

2 teaspoons paprika

large pinch of cayenne pepper

2 x 400g (14oz) cans of chopped tomatoes

400ml (14fl oz) chicken stock

a few sprigs of coriander, leaves and stems finely chopped

a few sprigs of flat leaf parsley, leaves and stems finely chopped

150g (5½oz) mature Cheddar cheese, grated

COUSCOUS

400g (14oz) couscous, cooked according to the packet instructions

75ml (5 tablespoons) olive oil

juice of 2 lemons

a few sprigs of soft herbs – flat leaf parsley, mint, coriander and chervil are all ideal, alone or a mixture, roughly chopped

To make the meatballs, heat a nonstick frying pan over a medium heat. Add a splash of olive oil, then the onion and garlic, season with salt and pepper and sauté for 4–5 minutes until softened but not coloured. Remove from the pan and let the onion mixture cool.

Mix the cooled onion mixture with the minced beef, harissa paste and breadcrumbs in a mixing bowl. Roll into balls about the size of a plum, then set aside for later.

Preheat the oven to 180°C fan (400°F), Gas Mark 6.

To make the sauce, heat a large saucepan over a medium heat and add a splash of olive oil. Add the onion and sauté for 4–5 minutes until softened but not coloured, then season with salt and pepper. Stir in the cumin, coriander, paprika and cayenne pepper, and cook together for 3–4 minutes. Pour in the chopped tomatoes and stock, bring to a simmer and cook for 15 minutes, then stir in the chopped coriander and parsley.

Next, heat a large nonstick frying pan over a medium heat. Add a little olive oil and fry the meatballs (in batches if necessary) so that they are nicely coloured all over. Transfer the meatballs to a large baking dish.

Pour the tomato sauce over the meatballs and scatter the Cheddar on top. Bake for 10 minutes so that the cheese is all melted and starting to colour.

Meanwhile, put the cooked couscous in a mixing bowl, add the olive oil, lemon juice and the herbs and mix in.

Serve a big bowl of the couscous and the meatball bake in the middle of the table and tuck in straight away.

SERVES 4

Preparation time 1 hour,
plus marinating
Cooking time 3½ hours

This is everything I want from a winter dish when it's freezing outside. It's decadent, indulgent and cries out for a bottle of red wine. Start this recipe the day before you want to cook.

Slow-cooked treacle ox cheek with celeriac dauphinoise & nutty crumble

3 tablespoons black treacle

4 chunks of ox cheek, about 350g (12oz) each, trimmed

vegetable oil, for cooking

1 onion, finely chopped

1 bay leaf

1 sprig of rosemary

500ml (18fl oz) stout

1 litre (1¾ pints) beef stock, or enough to cover

sea salt flakes and freshly ground black pepper

DAUPHINOISE

600ml (20fl oz) double cream

3 garlic cloves, peeled

1 sprig of rosemary

600g (1lb 5oz) fluffy-textured potatoes, such as Maris Piper, peeled and sliced 2mm (1/16-inch) thick

2 small celeriac, peeled and sliced 2mm (1/16-inch) thick

100g (3½oz) Parmesan cheese, finely grated

sea salt flakes and freshly ground black pepper

CRUMBLE

50g (1¾oz) rolled oats

20g (¾oz) butter

20g (¾oz) blanched hazelnuts

20g (¾oz) unsalted pistachios

pinch of sea salt flakes

a few sprigs of flat leaf parsley, leaves and stems finely chopped

The day before you want to cook, rub the treacle into the ox cheeks, cover and leave to marinate in the refrigerator overnight.

The next day, heat a flameproof casserole dish over a medium heat and add a drizzle of vegetable oil. Season the ox cheeks with salt and pepper, then add them to the pan and seal all over. Transfer to a plate. Reduce the heat, add the onion, bay leaf and rosemary and cook slowly for 10–12 minutes until softened. Season with salt and pepper.

Add the stout, increase the heat to high and reduce by three-quarters. Next, pour in the stock, return the sealed cheeks to the pan and bring to the boil. Reduce the heat to a gentle simmer, put a lid on the pan and cook for 3 hours. Discard the bay leaf and rosemary.

Meanwhile, make the dauphinoise. Preheat the oven to 160°C fan (350°F), Gas Mark 4.

Put the cream, garlic and rosemary in a saucepan over a low heat, and season with salt and pepper. Bring to a simmer, then remove from the heat and leave to infuse for 20 minutes. Strain the infused cream through a sieve into a large saucepan and discard the garlic and rosemary.

Add the sliced potato and celeriac to the cream, stir and bring to the boil. Once boiling, remove from the heat and transfer the contents to a baking dish about 20 x 10cm (8 x 4 inches). Gently press down the slices to create a level surface. Bake for 45 minutes, then remove from the oven and sprinkle the Parmesan evenly on top. Bake for a further 15 minutes.

To make the crumble, put all the ingredients except the parsley in a nonstick frying pan over a medium heat and cook for 5–6 minutes until golden brown. Remove from the heat and allow to cool, before pulsing in a blender to make a coarse crumble. Stir in the parsley.

Serve the ox cheek sprinkled with the nutty crumble, with a good spoon of the dauphinoise and plenty of gravy from the casserole dish.

Preparation time 30 minutes
Cooking time 2 hours 40 minutes,
plus resting

Definitely not a traditional risotto, but without doubt this is tasty! Using cream or mascarpone is sometimes considered a sin, but here it works really well with the barley and artichokes. If artichokes are not in season, substitute with new or Ratte potatoes.

Slow-roast pork belly with Jerusalem artichoke & pearl barley risotto

300g (10½oz) pearl barley

800g (1lb 12oz) boneless pork belly, skin scored every 1cm (½-inch)

60g (2¼oz) butter

2 onions, finely chopped

2 garlic cloves, finely chopped

1 sprig of thyme, leaves picked, plus extra for garnish

800g (1lb 12oz) Jerusalem artichokes, peeled and cut into 1cm (½-inch) pieces

850ml (1½ pints) chicken stock

2 tablespoons mascarpone cheese

80g (2¾oz) Parmesan cheese, finely grated

a few sprigs of flat leaf parsley, leaves and stems finely chopped

sea salt flakes and freshly ground black pepper

Cook the pearl barley according to the packet instructions and set aside.

Preheat the oven to 120°C fan (275°F), Gas Mark 1.

Season the pork belly all over with salt and pepper. Lay skin-side up on a wire rack set over a roasting tray and roast for 2½ hours. After this time the meat will be really tender and ready to crisp.

To crisp the skin, remove the pork from the oven and increase the oven temperature to its maximum. Once the oven has reached temperature, put the pork back in for about 10 minutes, but do keep an eye on it, as it can burn quickly. The skin will puff up, giving you the lightest crackling.

While the pork is in the oven for the long roast, with 30 minutes to go, prepare the risotto. Put the butter in a large saucepan over a medium heat. When it's starting to bubble, add the onions, garlic and thyme leaves, and season with salt and pepper. Reduce the heat and slowly sauté for 12–15 minutes until the onion has softened.

Add the artichokes, put a lid on the pan and sweat for 10 minutes. Once the 10 minutes are up, add the barley and chicken stock and stir in well. Simmer, uncovered, until the stock has almost all gone, before adding the mascarpone and stirring in well.

Once the crackling is crisp, remove the pork from the oven and let it rest while you finish the risotto. Add the Parmesan and the chopped parsley to the barley. Taste and check the seasoning one last time.

Once the pork has rested, carve into slices 2cm (¾-inch) thick and serve on top of a good spoon of the risotto.

Mussels are a brilliant dinner option and the sauce they make can't be beaten, especially when mopped up with lots of good bread.

Mussels in cider with leeks & tarragon

500g (1lb 2oz) fresh mussels

olive oil, for cooking

3 leeks, trimmed, cleaned and cut into rounds 1cm (½-inch) thick

2 garlic cloves, finely chopped

500ml (18fl oz) good-quality cider

100ml (3½fl oz) double cream

a few sprigs of tarragon, leaves finely chopped

sea salt flakes and freshly ground black pepper

First, clean the mussels by scrubbing the shells and pulling off the stringy beards, discarding any with broken shells.

Heat a splash of olive oil in a large flameproof casserole dish. Add the leeks and garlic, season with salt and pepper and sweat over a medium-low heat for 8–10 minutes until the leeks are soft but not coloured.

Pour in the cider, bring to the boil and reduce by half.

Next, add the mussels and put a lid on the pan. Increase the heat and cook for about 4 minutes until the mussels are open (discard any that remain closed).

Take the lid off, add the cream and tarragon and boil over a high heat until the sauce reduces a little. Serve in big bowls with plenty of the sauce.

SERVES 2

Preparation time 15 minutes
Cooking time 15 minutes

Summer time cries out for warm salads and this is one of my favourites. The green sauce is based on the classic Fergus Henderson recipe, but I've added a little mustard and some shallot to help the overall balance of the dish.

Warm salmon & potato salad with soft-boiled eggs & green sauce

280–300g (10–10½oz) skinless salmon fillet, as thick as possible

olive oil, for cooking

150g (5½oz) new potatoes, cooked and sliced 5mm (¼-inch) thick

2 eggs, cooked in salted boiling water for 6 minutes

sea salt flakes and freshly ground black pepper

GREEN SAUCE

a few sprigs of flat leaf parsley, leaves and stems finely chopped

a few sprigs of mint, leaves finely chopped

a few sprigs of dill, leaves and stems finely chopped

a few sprigs of tarragon, leaves and stems finely chopped

1 teaspoon Dijon mustard

3 anchovy fillets, finely chopped

1 shallot, finely chopped

1 garlic clove, finely chopped

1 tablespoon capers, rinsed and finely chopped

200ml (7fl oz) olive oil

sea salt flakes and freshly ground black pepper

Preheat an oven to 160°C fan (350°F), Gas Mark 4.

Line a baking sheet with baking parchment, add the salmon and drizzle a little olive oil over. Season with salt and pepper and bake for about 12 minutes so that it's cooked but still a little pink in the centre.

While the salmon is cooking, make the green sauce by mixing all the ingredients together in a mixing bowl.

In another mixing bowl, dress the new potatoes with 2 tablespoons of the green sauce and mix together well. Divide between 2 serving bowls.

When the salmon is ready, remove from the oven and gently flake the fish over the potatoes in the bowls.

Shell and halve the boiled eggs, then add 2 halves on top of each serving. Season the yolks with salt and pepper and serve with the green sauce. Any leftover sauce can be refrigerated for up to 2 days.

Wild garlic and Jersey Royals are ingredients that scream spring to me. If you can't find wild garlic, use a handful of spinach with 2 garlic cloves, blanched in salted boiling water for 30 seconds.

Baked cod with wild garlic pesto, new potatoes & peas

4 cod fillets, about 150g (5½oz) each, skinned and pin-boned

50ml (2fl oz) olive oil

25g (1oz) butter

300g (10½oz) waxy new potatoes (I use Jersey Royals), boiled until tender, then cut into 1cm (½-inch) thick slices

200ml (7fl oz) chicken stock

150g (5½oz) peas, preferably fresh, but frozen is fine, too

a few sprigs of mint, leaves finely chopped

sea salt flakes and freshly ground black pepper

WILD GARLIC PESTO

8–10 wild garlic leaves (keep any flowers that come with for garnish)

50ml (2fl oz) olive oil

50g (1¾oz) Parmesan cheese, grated

15g (½oz) pine nuts, toasted

sea salt flakes and freshly ground black pepper

To make the wild garlic pesto, bring a pan of salted water to the boil. Blanch the wild garlic leaves for 10 seconds, then drain and refresh in iced water. Drain well again and pat dry with kitchen paper.

Add the blanched wild garlic to a blender along with the olive oil, Parmesan and pine nuts, and blend until smooth. Season with salt and pepper and set aside until later.

Preheat the oven to 180°C fan (400°F), Gas Mark 6.

Line a baking sheet with baking parchment, add the cod fillets and drizzle over the olive oil. Season with salt and pepper and bake for 12 minutes.

Meanwhile, heat the butter in a saucepan over a medium heat and add the potatoes and the chicken stock. Once the stock starts to boil, add the peas and increase the heat to high. The stock will reduce into the butter and make an emulsion around the potatoes and peas. Once they are all glossy, turn off the heat and stir in the mint.

When the fish is ready, remove from the oven.

To serve, divide the potatoes and peas between 4 bowls and top with the cod. Finish with a good spoon of the wild garlic pesto on top.

If you have any wild garlic flowers, sprinkle them on top as a garnish.

Preparation time 20 minutes
Cooking time 1 hour

Using the coarse blade of a spiralizer means you'll get lovely spaghetti-like strands of potato, which is a great alternative to the heavier, traditional mashed potato topping.

Curried smoked haddock fish pie with crunchy potato topping

½ teaspoon cumin seeds

½ teaspoon coriander seeds

1 teaspoon curry powder

olive oil, for cooking

½ onion, finely chopped

1 small carrot, peeled and finely chopped

1 celery stick, finely chopped

1 green chilli, deseeded and finely chopped

1 bay leaf

200ml (7fl oz) chicken or vegetable stock

200ml (7fl oz) double cream

400g (14oz) smoked haddock, skinned and cut into 2cm (¾-inch) cubes

a few sprigs of coriander, leaves and stems roughly chopped

4 fluffy-textured potatoes (such as Maris Piper), peeled

30g (1oz) butter, melted

sea salt flakes and freshly ground black pepper

Preheat the oven to 180°C fan (400°F), Gas Mark 6.

Toast the cumin and coriander seeds with the curry powder in a small dry frying pan over a low heat for a couple of minutes, taking care not to burn. Set aside.

Pour a splash of olive oil in a large saucepan over a medium heat, add the onion, carrot, celery, chilli and bay leaf, and season with salt and pepper. Sweat for 6–7 minutes, taking care not to colour.

Add the toasted spices and stir in, then pour in the stock, increase the heat and bring to the boil. Continue cooking to reduce by three-quarters.

Once the stock has reduced, add the cream and continue cooking over a high heat to reduce by half.

Remove from the heat, add the haddock and coriander and stir in. Taste and check the seasoning. Transfer the haddock mixture to a pie dish about 20cm (8-inches) in diameter.

Using the coarse blade of a spiralizer, cut the potatoes into spaghetti strands. Toss them in the melted butter in a mixing bowl, and season with salt and pepper.

Lay out the spiralized potatoes over the haddock mixture, leaving plenty of volume so that they can crisp up nicely. Bake for 40 minutes – the top should be golden and crunchy.

Asian
barbecue
feast

Asian barbecue feast

I love a barbecue and cook food on it all year round.
Using Asian flavours – sticky glazes over caramelized meats,
subtle spices, lots of fresh herbs – is a favourite and works so well.
The flavour from a charcoal barbecue is fantastic, but if you don't
have one, use a griddle pan on the hob.

Chicken yakitori

MAKES 8

Preparation time 20 minutes
Cooking time 20 minutes

1 bunch of spring onions

80g (2¾oz) fresh root ginger, peeled
and cut into slices 5mm (¼-inch) thick

pinch of chilli flakes

200ml (7fl oz) soy sauce

200ml (7fl oz) mirin

8 large chicken thighs, boned and cut
into quarters

3 leeks, trimmed, cleaned and cut into
rounds 2cm (¾-inch) thick

vegetable oil, for oiling

If using wooden skewers, soak them in water for a few hours to prevent them burning.

First, separate the white and green parts of the spring onions. Finely chop the green parts, put them in a small bowl of cold water and keep in the refrigerator until ready to serve.

Chop the white parts into 2.5cm (1-inch) pieces and add to a saucepan with the ginger, chilli flakes, soy sauce and mirin, then bring to the boil. Reduce the heat to a simmer and reduce by three-quarters. Strain the glaze mixture through a sieve and set aside.

Thread 4 pieces of chicken on to each skewer, each piece alternating with a piece of leek so that you have 4 pieces of both on each skewer.

Lightly oil the skewered ingredients and, when ready to cook, put the skewers on the barbecue over a medium heat.

Once the meat is starting to brown on each side, brush the glaze over the chicken, turning and continuing to brush so that it's glazed on all sides. The sugar in the glaze will naturally caramelize and colour, so just keep brushing over and building up the glaze for 10 minutes or so. The chicken will be cooked after 15 minutes.

Serve with the drained chopped spring onion greens on top.

Five spice pork belly

SERVES 8

Preparation time 5 minutes,
plus marinating
Cooking time 3¼ hours

1kg (2lb 4oz) boneless pork belly,
skin scored every 1cm (½ inch)
2 tablespoons five spice powder
large pinch of sea salt flakes

Rub the pork belly with the five-spice and salt in a dish, cover and marinate in the refrigerator for 3 hours.

Preheat the oven to 130°C fan (300°F), Gas Mark 2.

Transfer the pork belly to a roasting tray and roast for 3 hours.

Remove the tray from the oven and let the pork cool enough to handle, then cut into long slices about 2cm (¾-inch) thick. Keep in the refrigerator until ready to serve.

When ready to serve, cook each piece on the barbecue for 15 minutes, turning halfway through, until coloured and nice and crisp – the skin should puff up and crackle.

Shrimp satay

MAKES 8

Preparation time 15 minutes,
plus marinating
Cooking time 15 minutes

32 raw peeled tiger prawns

SHRIMP MARINADE

2 tablespoons olive oil

juice of 1 lime

1 garlic clove, finely chopped

1 teaspoon ground cumin

1 teaspoon ground coriander

1 teaspoon ground turmeric

pinch of sea salt flakes

SATAY SAUCE

200g (7oz) raw blanched peanuts

40g (1½oz) light brown soft sugar

generous pinch of cayenne pepper

generous pinch of sea salt flakes

150ml (5fl oz) coconut milk

75ml (5 tablespoons) water

juice of 2 limes

2 tablespoons fish sauce

1 tablespoon sesame oil

First, mix together all the ingredients for the shrimp marinade in a bowl, add the prawns and mix well. Cover and marinate in the refrigerator for 3 hours.

To make the satay sauce, preheat the oven to 160°C (350°F), Gas Mark 4. Spread the peanuts out on a baking tray and toast for about 10 minutes, stirring halfway through, until golden brown. Remove from the oven and let them cool.

Put the toasted peanuts in a blender with the rest of the ingredients for the sauce and blitz together until smooth.

When ready to cook the prawns, thread 4 prawns on to each skewer and grill very quickly on the barbecue; 2 minutes on each side will be enough. Serve with the satay sauce on the side. Any leftover sauce can be stored in an airtight container in the refrigerator for up to 2 days.

Stir-fried pak choi with sticky shiitake mushrooms

SERVES 8

Preparation time 5 minutes
Cooking time 20 minutes

vegetable oil, for cooking

200g (7oz) shiitake mushrooms, stems removed and cut into slices 5mm (¼-inch) thick

1 tablespoon honey

2 tablespoons dark soy sauce

4 heads of pak choi, roots trimmed and leaves separated

30g (1oz) fresh root ginger, peeled and finely sliced

2 garlic cloves, finely sliced

Heat a splash of vegetable oil in a nonstick frying pan over a medium heat and sauté the mushrooms for about 8 minutes until they start to colour.

Add the honey and soy sauce and stir in well, then continue cooking until the mushrooms have absorbed all the liquid.

Turn off the heat and let the mushrooms cool.

Pour another splash of oil in a large frying pan or wok over a medium heat. Add the pak choi leaves, then the ginger and garlic on top and stir-fry for 5–6 minutes.

Add the sticky mushrooms, toss through and serve immediately.

Kimchi potato bake

SERVES 8

Preparation time 10 minutes
Cooking time 1 hour

4 spring onions

8–10 fluffy-textured potatoes, such as Maris Piper, peeled and cut into 2cm (¾-inch) pieces

vegetable oil, for cooking

pinch of sea salt flakes

100g (3½oz) good-quality kimchi

1 tablespoon white sesame seeds, toasted

1 tablespoon black sesame seeds, toasted

⅓ bunch (about 10g/¼oz) of coriander, roughly chopped

Preheat the oven to 200°C fan (425°F), Gas Mark 7.

First, separate the white and green parts of the spring onions. Finely slice the green parts, put them in a bowl of cold water and keep in the refrigerator until ready to serve.

Cut the white parts into 2.5cm (1-inch) pieces.

Put the potatoes in a roasting tray with a good splash of vegetable oil and season with the salt. Roast for 35 minutes until they start to colour.

Remove the tray from the oven, add the kimchi and spring onion whites and stir in well.

Return to the oven for another 15 minutes, then stir the ingredients again before roasting for a final 10 minutes.

Remove the bake from the oven and sprinkle over the drained spring onion greens, the toasted sesame seeds and coriander, before serving.

A lazy
Sunday
roast

A lazy Sunday roast

Sunday roasts are hugely important for me. They represent family and friends gathering together to feast on wonderful food, and in my opinion it's a great tradition. A roast is a meal we all cook to some degree, so I wanted to share a recipe for something a little different but still based on the idea of roasting a piece of meat. Lamb shoulder is a brilliant cut – cooked well, it just falls apart. When the meat is roasted over potatoes, none of the juices are allowed to escape and the flavour is immense. I like to eat around 2pm so that you have late morning to prepare, and then by late afternoon you're sitting on the sofa relaxing in a food coma.

Slow-cooked lamb shoulder with boulangère potatoes

SERVES 8

Preparation time 30 minutes
Cooking time 5 hours

BOULANGÈRE POTATOES

2kg (4lb 8oz) fluffy-textured potatoes, such as Maris Piper

5 onions

50g (1¾oz) butter, melted

1 litre (1¾ pints) chicken stock

sea salt flakes and freshly ground black pepper

Preheat an oven to 140°C fan (325°F), Gas Mark 3.

First prepare the boulangère potatoes. Peel the potatoes and then, using a mandolin, or a sharp knife if you don't have one, slice them about 5mm (¼-inch) thick. Peel and finely slice the onions.

Brush the base of a roasting tray big enough to hold the lamb with the melted butter. Spread over an even layer of potato slices, then scatter a layer of onions on top. Season with salt and pepper. Repeat the process until you have multiple layers of potato and onion, finishing with a layer of potato. The tray should be filled up to 2cm (¾-inch) from the top.

Pour over the chicken stock so that it comes about halfway up the potato layers and brush the top layer of potato slices with the rest of the butter.

Next, prepare the lamb. Mix the olive oil and rosemary together and rub into the lamb shoulder all over. Poke 4 holes into the lamb using a sharp knife and stud with the garlic cloves, then season all over with salt and pepper. Place the shoulder on top of the potatoes.

Roast for 4 hours, removing the tray from the oven and pushing the potatoes down with a palette knife every 30 minutes or so to keep them from drying out.

LAMB

50ml (2fl oz) olive oil

1 large sprig of rosemary, leaves picked and finely chopped

1 lamb shoulder, on the bone, about 2.2kg (4lb 13oz)

4 garlic cloves

sea salt flakes and freshly ground black pepper

GLAZE

500ml (18fl oz) lamb stock

2 tablespoons Marmite

1 tablespoon honey

Meanwhile, bring the ingredients for the glaze to the boil in a saucepan and reduce by half.

Once the 4 hours has passed, remove the lamb from the oven and increase the oven temperature to 180°C fan (400°F), Gas Mark 6.

Spoon over enough of the glaze to cover the surface of the lamb shoulder, then roast for a further 10 minutes.

Repeat this process 3 more times until all the glaze has been used up. The shoulder will have a nice shine to it.

Remove the tray from the oven and lift the shoulder out on to a plate to rest. Press the potatoes down one more time and return to the oven for about 20 minutes to colour all over.

When ready to serve, sit the lamb back on the potatoes and serve in the middle of the table, with the Green Beans with Brown Butter & Almonds (*see* page 145) on the side.

Green beans with brown butter & almonds

SERVES 8

Preparation time 5 minutes
Cooking time 10 minutes

80g (2¾oz) butter
50g (1¾oz) flaked almonds
juice of ½ lemon
1kg (2lb 4oz) green beans, trimmed
sea salt flakes and freshly ground black pepper

Bring a large saucepan of salted water to the boil.

Meanwhile, put the butter in a large nonstick frying pan and melt over a medium heat. Add the almonds and cook slowly until both the almonds and the butter are brown.

Turn off the heat and add the lemon juice while swirling the pan. It will spit a little, so do be careful. Set aside while you cook the beans.

Add the green beans to the salted boiling water and cook for 3 minutes.

Drain, then add to the buttery almonds and toss through. Season with salt and pepper.

Steak
night

Steak night

It's become clear that we all need to eat less meat and more vegetables and grains. In my home I've found we are eating less meat, but of much better quality. Eating good meat is so important, both for our health and for the livelihoods of the farmers producing it, and with that comes a higher price. I'd much rather spend a little extra and have a special, properly reared, well-aged piece of locally produced beef from my neighbourhood butcher once a week than average, poorly treated meat daily.

At home, we've made it a thing to have a proper steak night when we fancy it (roughly once a fortnight). We light the barbecue, whatever the weather, as cooking over coals makes a huge difference to the flavour. It's worth the extra time – crack open a beer, have some music on and show the meat the love it deserves. We tend to get a larger cut of beef to share, as having a thicker piece of meat gives you more control over the cooking. You can get a really good char on the outside without running the risk of overcooking the centre.

A good steak needs great sides, too. Spuds and béarnaise sauce are a given for me, while a luxurious creamed spinach rounds off the garnishes nicely. I've also started making bone marrow gravy at home and freezing it in batches so that we always have it to hand. It takes a while to prepare, but make it once and you'll reap the rewards.

Steak varieties and cooking tips

There's a lot of choice when it comes to selecting which cut to go for and that can be a decision based on price, flavour or tenderness. Here I've noted the best steaks to go for, with a few words on why.

If possible, do buy them from your local butcher, as you'll be able to see the cuts properly for yourself and get some expert advice from someone who lives and breathes meat. If you can't see what you're after, ask what they have in the back. Small retail spaces can mean that butchers can't display everything and I often find they have what I'm looking for in the chiller.

Remember, fat = flavour, so look for the steak with the best marbling you can find.

The steaks detailed below are all meant to be cooked over direct heat, preferably over coals (*see* method on page 150). But there's no reason why you can't slow-cook a piece of brisket or short rib and finish over the coals, too. These cuts will be a lot more economical, but they take longer to prepare and you do get a very different result, although still really tasty!

RIB-EYE

For me, the rib-eye steak is up there with the best. There's a big chunk of fat in the middle, meaning it needs to be cooked medium-rare at the minimum to break that fat down. The rib has the richest flavour due to the amount of fat running through it. You can get individual steaks or one extra-large steak for two people. If possible, buy it on the bone.

SIRLOIN

My other go-to steak, the sirloin has a layer of fat on the top side and a fairly lean piece of meat beneath. Another one that benefits from being cooked on the bone, I'd recommend this cut if you're after a great steak that's a little less rich than a rib-eye but still packed with flavour. Due to being slightly leaner, it's better cooked slightly less than medium-rare.

FILLET

Meat is muscle and the more it works, the tougher it will be. The fillet sits under the spine and hardly moves, making it by far the leanest cut. It doesn't have as much flavour as the rib or sirloin due to a lack of fat, but it melts in the mouth. I'd cook this for less time than any of the others, rare being my preference.

T-BONE/PORTERHOUSE

With this cut you can get the best of both worlds, having sirloin on one side and fillet on the other. The flavour of the sirloin and the tenderness of the fillet makes this cut very popular. One important thing to note when cooking – as the fillet needs to be cooked much less than the sirloin (not just because of the nature of the cut, but also the size difference), you'll want to whip the fillet off once it's cooked, then return the sirloin, still on the bone, to the grill to finish off. You can then put the fillet back in its place when you carve the whole thing and serve.

RUMP

The most economical of cuts, the rump has great flavour but can be a little tougher. I'd cook this closer to rare, and try to get a larger piece to share so that you can get a good char.

When cooking a feast for eight, I'd suggest, if possible, buying a few different cuts so that you can have some variety. I work on around 300g (10½oz) meat (raw weight) per person. That doubles up to 600g (1lb 5oz) and so on for larger cuts to be shared. If there's a bone, allow 100–150g (3½–5½oz) extra weight per steak.

Pan-fried steak

Preparation time none
Cooking time see method, plus
10–30 minutes resting

1kg (2lb 4oz) bone-in rib eye steak

1kg (2lb 4oz) bone-in sirloin steak

vegetable oil

knob of butter

sprig of rosemary

handful of garlic cloves, bashed

sea salt flakes and freshly ground
black pepper

Allow the steaks to come up to room temperature 30 minutes–1 hour before cooking. Season all over with salt and pepper.

Preheat the oven to 180°C fan (400°F), Gas Mark 6.

Heat a large skillet or ovenproof frying pan over a high heat and add a splash of vegetable oil. Sear the steaks on both sides, then transfer the pan to the oven. For larger cuts like these, I use a meat thermometer to check if the steaks are cooked: rare 40°C (104°F); medium-rare 55°C (131°F); medium 60°C (140°F); medium-well 65°C (149°F), well-done 70°C (158°F). Smaller cuts (less than 1 inch thick), won't need cooking in the oven and I use my fingers to feel how the firmness changes through the cooking to tell when they are ready – the firmer it feels, the more it's cooked – this takes a lot of practice.

Once the steaks are a few degrees below the target temperature or when the smaller cuts are sealed, add the butter to the pan along with the rosemary and garlic. Once the butter starts foaming, baste the steak continually for 4–5 minutes or until cooked, moving on to the heat if the butter gets too cold or off the heat if it gets too hot. Transfer the steaks to a wire rack to rest for at least 30 minutes (or 10–15 minutes for smaller cuts) – this is to allow the meat to relax and to stop the juices leaking out when you cut into it. When ready to serve always carve against the grain.

Chipped potatoes with rosemary & garlic

SERVES 8

Preparation time 10 minutes
Cooking time 1 hour

100ml (3½fl oz) olive oil

1 large sprig of rosemary, leaves picked

5 garlic cloves, unpeeled

2kg (4lb 8oz) fluffy-textured potatoes, such as Maris Piper

sea salt flakes and freshly ground
black pepper

Preheat the oven to 180°C fan (400°F), Gas Mark 6.

Put the olive oil, rosemary and garlic in a large roasting tray and season with salt and pepper.

Peel the potatoes and cut into 2–3cm (¾–1¼-inch) chunks – they can be a bit random-shaped. Add to the roasting tray and toss all together with your hands.

Roast for 50 minutes–1 hour until they are lovely and golden, crisp on the outside and cooked in the centre. You want to turn them in the tray every 10 minutes or so. If they break down a little when you turn them, that's OK – the broken pieces will be the parts that get really crisp and taste wonderful.

Béarnaise sauce

SERVES 8

Preparation time 5 minutes
Cooking time 10 minutes

250g (9oz) salted butter

2 egg yolks

2 tablespoons white wine vinegar

2 tablespoons water

½ packet (about 15g/½oz) tarragon, leaves finely chopped

sea salt flakes and freshly ground black pepper

Melt the butter in a small saucepan over a low heat, skimming off the milky parts. You only want the fat.

Heat another pan of water, over which a heatproof mixing bowl can be set without the base touching the water, until simmering.

Put the egg yolks, vinegar and measured water in your heatproof bowl, then whisk together over the pan of water until light and fluffy. If the egg yolks start to cook too quickly, reduce the heat or remove the bowl from the heat.

Once the mixture is fluffy, remove the bowl from the heat and start to whisk in the butter gradually. If the mixture becomes too thick, add 1 teaspoon of warm water, then go back to adding the butter as you were.

When all the butter has been incorporated, season with salt and pepper and stir in the chopped tarragon when ready to serve.

Bone marrow gravy

SERVES 8

Preparation time 10 minutes
Cooking time 9½ hours

2kg (4lb 8oz) beef bones
1kg (2lb 4oz) marrowbones – ask your butcher to split them in half
1 onion, halved
2 carrots, peeled and halved lengthways
vegetable oil, for cooking
1 sprig of rosemary
1 bay leaf
375ml (13fl oz) red wine

TO FINISH

5 shallots, finely chopped
a few sprigs of thyme
a few sprigs of rosemary
2 bay leaves
100ml (3½fl oz) port
finely chopped flat leaf parsley

Preheat the oven to 180°C fan (400°F), Gas Mark 6.

In 2 separate roasting trays, roast both the beef bones and marrowbones for about 40 minutes (or longer if they're large), until the marrow is cooked and the beef bones are dark brown.

Remove the trays from the oven and transfer the beef bones to a large stock pot. Fill with cold water to just cover and bring to a simmer. Skim off any fat that comes off and discard.

While the stock is simmering, scoop out the marrowbone flesh and set aside in the refrigerator. Put the bones in the pot with the others.

Meanwhile, add the onion and carrots to another roasting tray and toss in a little vegetable oil. Roast for 30–40 minutes, until browned.

Remove the tray from the oven and add the roasted veg to the bones in the pot, along with the rosemary and bay leaf. Pour in the red wine and continue simmering, uncovered, for 8 hours, occasionally skimming off any fat.

Once the cooking time is up, strain the stock through a fine sieve.

Place another saucepan over a medium heat and pour in a drizzle of vegetable oil. Add the shallots with the thyme, rosemary and bay leaves, then reduce the heat and sweat for 15–20 minutes, until the shallots are translucent.

Pour in the port, increase the heat and reduce by three-quarters. Add the beef stock and reduce until you have a gravy-like consistency.

Pick out the herb sprigs, leaving the shallots in. Chop the roasted marrow flesh and stir it in. Finish by stirring in the chopped parsley at the last moment.

Blue cheese creamed spinach

SERVES 8

Preparation time 15 minutes
Cooking time 15 minutes

knob of butter
1 onion, finely chopped
2 garlic cloves, finely chopped
200ml (7fl oz) double cream
500g (1lb 2oz) spinach, washed
80g (2¾oz) blue cheese (I use Stilton)
sea salt flakes and freshly ground
black pepper

Put the butter in a saucepan and melt over a medium heat. Then add the onion and garlic and sweat for 6–8 minutes without colouring.

Pour in the cream, bring to the boil and reduce by half, then turn off the heat and set aside. Season with salt and pepper.

Bring a pan of water to the boil and blanch the spinach for 30 seconds. Drain and refresh in iced water, then drain again, squeezing out as much of the water as possible.

Add the spinach to the cream mixture and stir until evenly coated.

Transfer from the pan to an ovenproof dish and crumble the blue cheese over. When ready to serve, reheat under a grill preheated to medium for 3 minutes, increasing the heat to high for the last 1–2 minutes to colour.

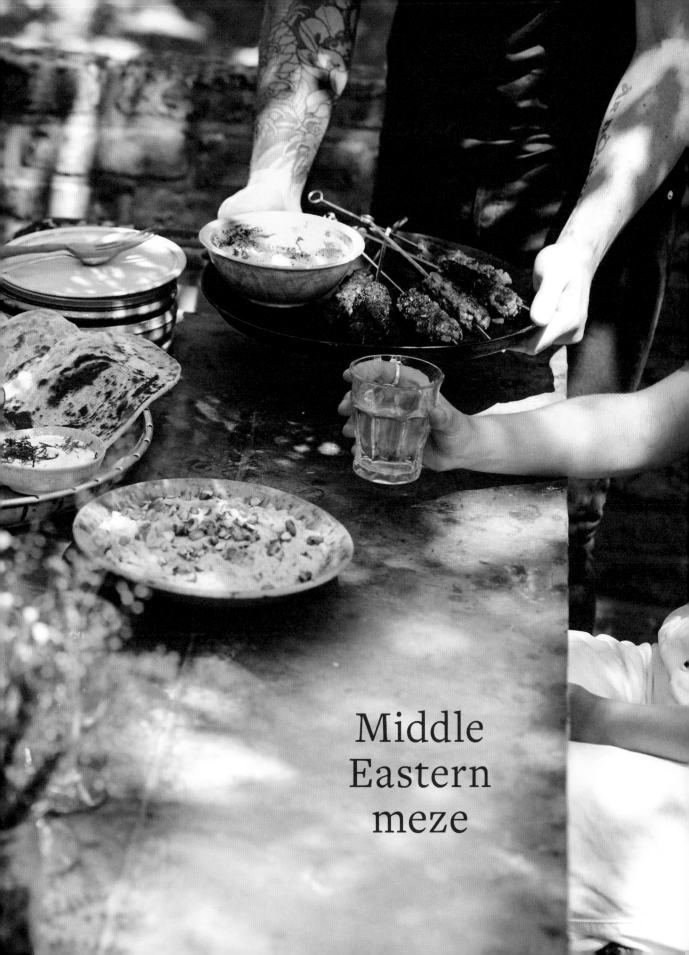

Middle
Eastern
meze

Middle Eastern meze

Middle Eastern food is my go-to when I'm stuck for ideas and it lends itself to a more informal feast – lots of little dishes in the middle of the table with plenty of bread to tear into is a wonderful way to eat. The griddle bread recipe in this feast is inspired by an Indian paratha and is an incredibly rich and moreish bread. Smoked yogurt is another of my favourite things to serve – people seem to love it and it goes with just about everything. You'll need a hot-smoker for that recipe, or you can set up your own form of smoker by following the instructions on page 158.

Do try and find the Middle Eastern herb-and-spice mix za-atar, which I use with roasted beetroots – it adds a brilliant burst of flavour.

Scale up all the recipes to make extra for lunch the next day, too.

Smoky baba ganoush

SERVES 8

Preparation time 5 minutes
Cooking time 30 minutes

4 aubergines

4 tablespoons tahini

2 garlic cloves, finely chopped

a few sprigs of flat leaf parsley, leaves and stems finely chopped

a few sprigs of mint, leaves finely chopped

50ml (2fl oz) olive oil, plus extra for drizzling

juice of 2 lemons

100g (3½oz) chopped pistachios

sea salt flakes and freshly ground black pepper

Over the coals of a barbecue, or the flame of a gas hob, blacken the aubergines until smoky and burned all over. By the time they are entirely charred, the aubergines will be softened and cooked inside. Set aside until cool enough to handle, then use a spoon to scoop out the flesh into a sieve and let it drain for 20 minutes

Roughly chop the aubergine flesh and put into a mixing bowl. Add all the other ingredients except the pistachios, season with salt and pepper and stir.

Serve in a bowl, with a drizzle of olive oil and the pistachios scattered on top.

Smoked yogurt with fresh herbs

SERVES 8

Preparation time 5 minutes,
plus chilling
Cooking time 25 minutes

500g (1lb 2oz) full-fat Greek yogurt
handful of smoking chips

TO SERVE
olive oil, for drizzling
a few sprigs of dill, leaves and stems finely chopped
a few sprigs of mint, leaves finely chopped
a few sprigs of flat leaf parsley, leaves and stems
finely chopped
freshly ground black pepper

Set up a hot-smoker with the smoking chips in the base, and when the smoke is coming through, smoke the yogurt for 15 minutes.

If you don't have a smoker, put the smoking chips in a large saucepan and place a stainless steel perforated vegetable steamer basket inside. Put the yogurt in a heatproof dish that's a bit smaller than the basket to let the smoke pass through, and then pop it into the basket. Cover the pan with a tight-fitting lid made of foil. Place the covered pan over a medium heat and, when you smell the smoke, reduce the heat and leave to smoke for 10 minutes. Remove from the heat and peel off the lid.

Remove the yogurt from the smoker and whisk back together; it may have separated a little and there will be a thin brown film on top, which is where all the flavour is, so make sure it gets mixed in well.

Cover and put in the refrigerator for a few hours to firm up a bit. Serve the yogurt with a drizzle of olive oil over the top, the fresh herbs sprinkled over and a twist of black pepper.

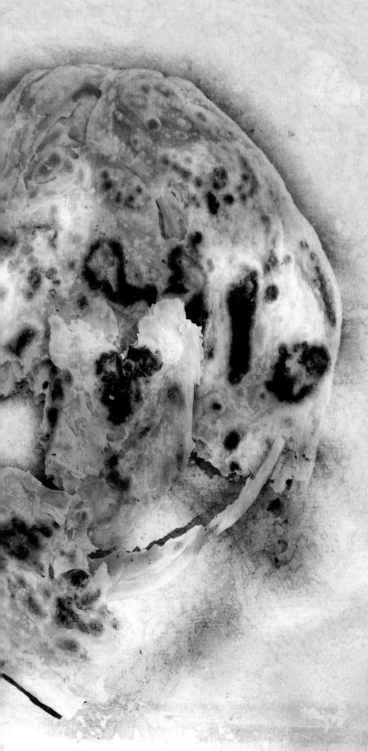

Griddle bread

MAKES 8

Preparation time 20 minutes,
plus resting
Cooking time 6 minutes per bread

100g (3½oz) butter, melted, for rolling and cooking

DOUGH
425g (15oz) plain flour, plus extra for dusting
90g (3¼oz) butter, melted
200ml (7fl oz) water
1 teaspoon sea salt flakes

Put all the ingredients for the dough in a mixing bowl and mix together to form a dough.

Knead the dough in the bowl for 5 minutes, then let it rest at room temperature, covered with a clean tea towel, for 4 hours.

Divide the dough into 8 balls and roll out each about 1mm ($\frac{1}{32}$-inch) thick.

Brush each with melted butter, then roll into a cigar shape. Next, roll up along its length into a snail-like shape. Then carefully roll out again 2mm ($\frac{1}{16}$-inch) thick.

Heat a nonstick frying pan over a medium heat and brush with 1 tablespoon of butter, then cook the breads, one at a time, for about 3 minutes on each side until starting to turn golden brown. If the bread burns slightly in areas, that's OK – it will bubble up a bit due to the layers created through rolling, and these bubbles may colour a little more quickly. Leave to cool on a wire rack.

Lentil & feta salad with parsley & pomegranate

Serves 8

Preparation time 10 minutes
Cooking time none

50ml (2fl oz) olive oil
50ml (2fl oz) sherry vinegar
pinch of chilli flakes
500g (1lb 2oz) cooked, ready-to-eat Puy lentils
a few sprigs of flat leaf parsley, leaves and stems finely chopped
100g (3½oz) feta cheese, crumbled
seeds of 1 pomegranate
sea salt flakes and freshly ground black pepper

Whisk together the olive oil, vinegar and chilli flakes in a mixing bowl.

Add the lentils, parsley and half the feta and stir. Season with salt and pepper.

Transfer to a serving dish and sprinkle the rest of the feta on top along with the pomegranate seeds.

Roasted beetroots with za'atar

Serves 8

Preparation time 10 minutes, plus cooling
Cooking time 1 hour 25 minutes

8–10 raw beetroots, a mixture of colours if possible, peeled
100ml (3½fl oz) olive oil
50ml (2fl oz) sherry vinegar
2 tablespoons za'atar
sea salt flakes and freshly ground black pepper
a few sprigs of oregano, leaves picked

Preheat the oven to 180°C fan (400°F), Gas Mark 6.

Cut the beetroots into wedges, getting about 10 from each.

Place the beetroot wedges in a roasting tray with the olive oil, vinegar and za'atar and season with salt and pepper. Mix together. Cover the tray with foil and roast for 1 hour 25 minutes, though check after 45 minutes as depending on the size of your beetroots they may cook more quickly - a knife should go through to the middle easily.

Remove the tray from the oven, lift off the foil and let the beetroots cool. Serve on a plate with the oregano leaves sprinkled over.

Butter bean hummus

Serves 8

Preparation time 10 minutes
Cooking time none

250g (9oz) drained canned butter beans
125g (4½oz) tahini
150ml (5fl oz) cold water
3 tablespoons lemon juice
1 garlic clove, finely chopped
sea salt flakes and freshly ground black pepper

TO SERVE
olive oil, for drizzling
a few sprigs of thyme, leaves picked
pinch of sumac

Blitz all the main ingredients together in a food processor or blender until smooth. Season with salt and pepper.

Serve in a bowl with olive oil drizzled over and the thyme leaves and sumac sprinkled on top.

Lamb kofte with apricots & pine nuts

Serves 8

Preparation time 10 minutes
Cooking time 20 minutes

75ml (5 tablespoons) olive oil
1 onion, finely chopped
3 garlic cloves, finely chopped
1 tablespoon cumin seeds
1 teaspoon chilli flakes
800g (1lb 12oz) minced lamb
a few sprigs of flat leaf parsley, leaves and stems finely chopped
80g (2¾oz) ready-to-eat dried apricots, finely chopped
vegetable oil, for cooking
sea salt flakes and freshly ground black pepper

Heat the olive oil in a frying pan over a medium heat. Add the onion, garlic, cumin seeds and chilli flakes and cook for 10–12 minutes, until the onion is soft and translucent. Season with salt and pepper and let the onion mixture cool.

Put the minced lamb, the cooled onion mixture, parsley and apricots in a mixing bowl and mix together well.

Divide the lamb mixture into 8 and shape each portion into a sausage. Thread each kofte on to a metal skewer, and when ready to cook, prepare a barbecue or heat a griddle pan on the hob.

Drizzle a little vegetable oil over each kofte and season with salt and pepper. Cook over a medium heat for 8–10 minutes, turning every few minutes, until nicely coloured all over on the outside and cooked in the middle.

Shellfish
supper

Shellfish supper

When I was 23 I spent 3 weeks on the West Coast of America
travelling and catching-up with some friends who had moved there.
The one meal that has always stuck in my mind was in Seattle.
I was with a friend and I don't really know why we ended up eating
in this particular place or what the speciality was; we just kind of
stumbled upon the restaurant one night. We saw the table next to us
receive their "pot"; the waiter arrived with a cauldron-like vessel,
tipped the entire contents on to the table and walked off. The diners
each had a mallet and a pick along with a bib and immediately got
stuck in. We ordered the same thing right away and it was incredibly
tasty and fun to eat. I started recreating this at home a few years ago
and it always goes down a storm. It's one of those roll-your-sleeves-
up-and-get-stuck-in kind of dishes that I just adore.

All-in-one seafood feast with corn on the cob, chorizo & sweet potato

SERVES 8

Preparation time 25 minutes
Cooking time 1½ hours

200g (7oz) butter

1 onion, finely chopped

3 garlic cloves, finely chopped

1 red chilli, finely chopped

2 tablespoons smoked paprika

500ml (18fl oz) chicken stock

1kg (2lb 4oz) sweet potatoes, peeled and cut into 3cm (1¼-inch) dice

50ml (2fl oz) vegetable oil

1 teaspoon Cajun seasoning

8 raw, if possible, or cooked crab claws in the shell, cracked

500g (1lb 2oz) cooked crayfish in the shell

24 raw tiger prawns in the shell

500g (1lb 2oz) fresh mussels, cleaned (*see* page 120)

500g (1lb 2oz) fresh clams, washed in cold water (discard any with broken shells)

200g (7oz) cooking chorizo sausage, sliced into rounds 2cm (¾-inch) thick

4 corn on the cob, husks and silky threads removed, halved and blanched in salted boiling water for 4 minutes

a few sprigs of parsley, finely chopped

sea salt flakes and freshly ground black pepper

Melt half the butter in a large saucepan over a medium heat. Add the onion, garlic and chilli and sauté for 10–12 minutes until the onion is soft. Then add the paprika and cook for another 3–4 minutes.

Pour in the chicken stock, bring to the boil and reduce by half, then set aside for later.

Preheat the oven to 180°C fan (400°F), Gas Mark 6.

Put the sweet potatoes and the vegetable oil in a large roasting tray and season with the Cajun seasoning, salt and pepper. Toss all together and roast for 45 minutes.

Meanwhile, melt the rest of the butter in large flameproof casserole dish over a medium heat. Add the crab claws and roast slowly on the hob for 5–6 minutes if they're raw, otherwise skip this step.

Next, add the crayfish, prawns, mussels, clams and reduced chicken stock and toss everything together. Pop a lid on the pan and cook for 6 minutes, then turn off the heat and set aside. If using cooked crab claws add them now.

Remove the sweet potatoes from the oven, sprinkle over the chorizo and add the corn. Toss together and roast for a further 15 minutes.

Remove the tray from the oven and pour the shellfish mixture and pan juices on top – you may need a second roasting tray to spread the bulk. Loosely toss all the elements together as best you can in the tray.

Return to the oven for a final 10 minutes, then finish by sprinkling with the parsley. Serve everything together.

Garlic cornbread

SERVES 8

Preparation time 10 minutes
Cooking time 40 minutes

600g (1lb 5oz) cornmeal

200g (7oz) plain flour

3 teaspoons baking powder

1½ teaspoons bicarbonate of soda

15g (½oz) sea salt flakes

3 eggs

150ml (¼ pint) buttermilk

450ml (16fl oz) whole milk

30g butter

4 garlic cloves, peeled and bashed

a bunch (about 30g/1oz) coriander, leaves and stems finely chopped

265g (9½oz) canned sweetcorn kernels, drained

3 jalapeno peppers, finely chopped

1 red onion, peeled and finely chopped

Mix the cornmeal, flour, baking powder, bicarbonate of soda and salt together in a large mixing bowl.

In a separate bowl, mix together the eggs, buttermilk and milk.

Add the egg mixture to the flour mixture and whisk until it becomes a smooth batter. Stir in the coriander, sweetcorn, peppers and onion.

Preheat the oven to 180°C fan (400°F), Gas Mark 6.

Heat a large skillet or ovenproof dish lined with baking parchment over a medium heat. Add the butter and the garlic to the skillet or dish. Reduce the heat to low and let the garlic infuse for 8–10 minutes.

Increase the heat to medium and let the garlic start to colour. At this stage, remove the garlic and pour in the cornbread batter. Reduce the heat to low again and cook for 5 minutes.

Transfer the skillet or dish to the oven and bake for 20 minutes until set in the middle. Remove the cornbread from the skillet or dish and leave to cool on a wire rack.

Cajun-spiced mayo

SERVES 8

Preparation time 10 minutes
Cooking time none

2 egg yolks
1 tablespoon Cajun seasoning
1 tablespoon Dijon mustard
50ml (2fl oz) white wine vinegar
400ml (14fl oz) groundnut oil
finely grated zest and juice of ½ lime
sea salt flakes

Blend the egg yolks, Cajun seasoning, mustard and vinegar together in a blender, or use an electric hand whisk.

Very slowly start adding the groundnut oil while the blender is running. If the mixture doesn't continue to blend together, add the oil more slowly.

Continue to blend in the oil until it's all incorporated. If the mixture becomes too thick and excessively greasy, add some warm water, 1 teaspoon at a time, until it loosens up a bit.

Season with salt and then mix in the lime zest and juice.

One-pot wonders

Preparation time 15 minutes
Cooking time 50 minutes

I first made this a few days after our daughter was born. We couldn't really do much, so chucking a load of veggies in the oven with some seasonings was easy – plus it got some much-needed nutrients into us!

Courgette, aubergine & pepper tray roast with garlic griddled bread

2 courgettes, sliced into rounds 1cm (½-inch) thick

1 aubergine, halved lengthways and sliced into half-rounds 1cm (½-inch) thick

2 red peppers, cored, deseeded and sliced into strips 1cm (½-inch) thick

2 plum tomatoes, quartered

1 tablespoon fennel seeds

2 garlic cloves, crushed

2 sprigs of rosemary

pinch of chilli flakes

100ml (3½fl oz) olive oil

a few sprigs of basil, leaves picked

80g (2¾oz) Parmesan cheese, grated

sea salt flakes and freshly ground black pepper

GARLIC GRIDDLED BREAD

2 garlic cloves, peeled

50ml (2fl oz) olive oil

2 large slices of sourdough bread

sea salt flakes and freshly ground black pepper

Preheat the oven to 180°C fan (400°F), Gas Mark 6. Put all the vegetables in a large roasting tray along with the fennel seeds, garlic, rosemary, chilli flakes and olive oil. Season with salt and pepper and give everything a good toss to mix.

Roast for 40 minutes – the veggies will be soft and nicely coloured.

Remove the tray from the oven and stir in the whole basil leaves. Sprinkle the Parmesan over and pop back in the oven for another 10 minutes.

To make the garlic griddled bread, blitz the garlic with the olive oil in a blender, then season with salt and pepper.

Pour the oil mixture on to a plate and coat the slices of bread in the oil.

Heat a griddle pan over a medium-high heat and griddle the bread on both sides so that it's nicely charred. Season with a little salt.

Serve the tray roast with the bread on the side, or spoon it on top of the bread.

I always double this and stick some in the freezer; it makes a great late-night supper when you have no time to cook. Serve with boiled rice or naan breads.

Squash & sweet potato curry with chickpeas & spinach

2 sweet potatoes, peeled and cut into 2cm (¾-inch) cubes

1 butternut squash, peeled, deseeded and cut into 2cm (¾-inch) cubes

vegetable oil, for cooking

1 onion, peeled and quartered

50g (1¾oz) fresh root ginger, peeled and roughly chopped

3 garlic cloves, peeled

2 hot red chillies

1 tablespoon cumin seeds

1 tablespoon ground coriander

400g (14oz) can of chickpeas, drained and rinsed

400g (14oz) can of chopped tomatoes

200ml (7fl oz) vegetable stock

400ml (14fl oz) can of coconut milk

260g (9½oz) baby spinach, washed

½ packet (about 15g/½oz) of coriander, leaves and stems roughly chopped

sea salt flakes and freshly ground black pepper

Preheat an oven to 200°C fan (425°F), Gas Mark 7.

Put the sweet potatoes and butternut squash in a large flameproof casserole dish and season with salt and pepper. Toss the vegetables in a little vegetable oil and roast in the oven for 40 minutes, stirring every 10 minutes.

Meanwhile, put the onion, ginger, garlic and chillies in a blender and blend until smooth.

Remove the pan from the oven, spoon out the roasted sweet potatoes and squash and set aside.

Add a touch more oil to the pan, place on the hob over a medium heat and toast the cumin and ground coriander for a minute or so, then add the onion mixture and sauté for 5–6 minutes.

Season with salt and pepper, then add the chickpeas, chopped tomatoes and vegetable stock. Stir, then simmer for 15 minutes.

Stir in the roasted sweet potatoes and squash, then pour in the coconut milk and bring to the boil. Reduce the heat and simmer for 5 minutes.

Add the spinach to the curry and cook until wilted. Finally, stir in the coriander and check the seasoning before serving.

SERVES 4

Preparation time 20 minutes
Cooking time 2 hours

A bit different to a traditional Sunday roast, this recipe is much easier and makes much less washing-up! You'll need a large casserole dish or a big roasting tray for this.

One-pot Sunday chicken

5 fluffy-textured medium potatoes, such as Maris Piper, halved

1 large chicken, about 2kg (4lb 8oz)

1 lemon, halved

4 garlic cloves, peeled and bashed

1 large sprig of thyme

3 carrots, peeled and halved lengthways

3 shallots, halved lengthways

100ml (3½fl oz) olive oil

2 Little Gem lettuces, quartered

500ml (18fl oz) chicken stock

30g (1oz) butter

2 handfuls of fresh or frozen peas

sea salt flakes and freshly ground black pepper

Preheat an oven to 200°C fan (425°F), Gas Mark 7.

Blanch the potatoes in boiling water for a few minutes, then drain.

Stuff the chicken with the lemon halves, garlic cloves and thyme and season all over with salt and pepper.

Put the chicken in a large flameproof casserole dish (or a big roasting tray), then arrange the potatoes, carrots and shallots around the outside.

Drizzle the olive oil all over the chicken and the vegetables, and season the veg with salt and pepper. Roast for 1 hour 20 minutes.

Remove from the oven, add the Little Gem quarters in and around the chicken and pour in the chicken stock, avoiding the chicken so that the skin stays crisp.

Reduce the oven temperature to 180°C fan (400°F), Gas Mark 6 and return the dish (or tray) to the oven for another 30 minutes.

When ready, remove from the oven and lift the chicken out on to a plate to rest. Remove the vegetables and arrange on a serving platter.

Pop the pot (or tray) on the hob and bring the contents to the boil. Reduce the sauce until it's a gravy-like consistency, skimming off the fat as you go.

Next, whisk in the butter to enrich the sauce. Then add the peas and cook for 2–3 minutes.

When the chicken is cool enough to handle, cut off the legs and the breasts and place on top of the veggies on the platter.

Serve up with a little of the sauce poured over and offer the rest in a jug on the side.

Preparation time 20 minutes
Cooking time 3¼ hours

A bit like baking dumplings on top of a stew, the scone topping gives a great crust while retaining lovely soft centres; perfect for mopping up the juices!

Barbecue spiced beef stew with a Cheddar & buttermilk scone topping

500g (1lb 2oz) beef chuck steak, diced

vegetable oil, for cooking

2 onions, finely chopped

2 carrots, peeled and cut into 1cm (½-inch) dice

2 garlic cloves, finely chopped

1 sprig of rosemary

1 tablespoon tomato purée

1 tablespoon plain flour

500ml (18fl oz) beef stock

sea salt flakes and freshly ground black pepper

BARBECUE SEASONING

3 tablespoons smoked paprika

1 tablespoon onion powder

1 tablespoon garlic powder

2 tablespoons sea salt flakes

3 tablespoons caster sugar

CHEDDAR & BUTTERMILK SCONES

10g (⅛oz) fresh yeast or 2 x 7g sachets fast-action dried yeast

300g (10½oz) plain flour, plus extra for dusting

150g (5½oz) butter, softened

150g (5½oz) Cheddar cheese, grated

20g (¾oz) chives, finely chopped

large pinch of sea salt flakes

200ml (7fl oz) buttermilk

4 egg yolks

2 eggs, beaten, to glaze

Mix all the barbecue seasoning ingredients together in a bowl, then use it to lightly coat the diced beef – any leftover seasoning mix can be stored in an airtight container.

Heat a good splash of vegetable oil in a flameproof casserole dish over a high heat and sear the beef so that it gets some good colour all over. Transfer the meat to a plate and set aside.

Add a drizzle more oil to the pan and sweat the onions, carrots, garlic and rosemary over a medium heat for 8–10 minutes without colouring too much. Season with salt and pepper.

Add the tomato purée and cook for 3–4 minutes. Then return the beef to the pan, sprinkle the flour over the top and stir in so that it's all coated nicely. Pour in the beef stock and bring to the boil, then reduce the heat and simmer, with the lid on, for 2½ hours, removing the lid for the final 30 minutes.

While the stew is cooking, make the scones. In a small bowl, mix the fresh (or dried) yeast with 1 tablespoon water. If using dried yeast, also add a pinch of sugar. Stir to dissolve and set aside.

Put the flour in the bowl of a stand mixer fitted with a dough hook. Rub the butter into the flour using your fingertips, then add half the Cheddar, the chives and salt until well combined. Add the buttermilk and egg yolks, and mix together on a low speed until a dough forms.

Roll out the dough on a lightly floured work surface until 4cm (1½-inches) thick, then cut out rounds with a 6cm (2½-inch) cutter. Put the scones on to a lined baking sheet and chill in the refrigerator until needed.

Preheat an oven to 180°C fan (400°F), Gas Mark 6.

When the stew is ready, take off the lid and check the seasoning one more time. Carefully arrange the scones on top, then brush with the beaten egg and sprinkle the rest of grated Cheddar over the top. Bake for 15 minutes, then serve.

SERVES 4

Preparation time 10 minutes,
plus marinating
Cooking time 3½ hours

Sticky glazed beef short ribs is one of my favourite dishes; the balance of sweet and salty together with the flavours of the chilli and ginger are just amazing. I think this is best served over steamed rice.

Japanese beef short ribs

2kg (4lb 8oz) beef short ribs, on the bone, cut into 4–6 chunks

vegetable oil, for cooking

1 litre (1¾ pints) beef stock

MARINADE

75ml (5 tablespoons) soy sauce

3 tablespoons dark brown sugar

pinch of sea salt flakes

10 garlic cloves, peeled

80g (2¾oz) fresh ginger root, peeled and cut into slices 5mm (¼-inch) thick

4 star anise

2 large red chillies, roughly chopped (with seeds)

2 bunches of spring onions, cut into rounds 1cm (½-inch) thick

100ml (3½fl oz) mirin

2 tablespoons red miso paste

TO SERVE

1 teaspoon white sesame seeds, toasted

1 teaspoon black sesame seeds, toasted

3 spring onions, chopped as finely as possible

For the marinade, mix all the ingredients together in a saucepan and bring to the boil, until the sugar and miso paste have dissolved.

Turn off the heat and let the marinade cool, then pour over the beef in a bowl, cover and marinate in the refrigerator overnight.

Preheat the oven to 140°C fan (325°F), Gas Mark 3.

Heat a flameproof casserole dish over a medium heat and add a splash of vegetable oil.

Lift the beef out of the marinade and pat dry with kitchen paper. Add to the pan and seal all over until nicely caramelized. Due to the sugar, it will colour quite quickly, so do keep an eye on it.

Pour over the marinade, along with the beef stock. Bring to the boil, then pop a lid on and transfer to the oven for 3 hours until the meat is falling off the bone.

When ready, remove the dish from the oven, take off the lid and lift the beef out on to a plate. Using a slotted spoon, scoop out the spring onions and the other bits in the marinade and discard.

Bring the stock mixture back to the boil on the hob and reduce until thickened to a gravy-like consistency, skimming off the fat as you go.

When the consistency is correct, return the chunks of beef to get them nicely glazed.

Sprinkle over the toasted sesame seeds and spring onions and serve straight away.

Preparation time 15 minutes,
plus soaking
Cooking time 3¼ hours, plus resting

Beans absorb liquid as they cook, so cooking the pork on top of the beans means that all the juices and flavours aren't wasted – the beans take it all in and taste fantastic.

Pot-roast pork belly, black beans & mojo verde

500g (1lb 2oz) dried black beans, soaked in cold water overnight and then drained

1 onion, finely chopped

3 garlic cloves, finely chopped

1 sprig of rosemary

3 bay leaves

2 chipotle chillies in adobo sauce

400g (14oz) can of chopped tomatoes

500ml (18fl oz) chicken stock

1kg (2lb 4oz) boneless pork belly, skin scored every 1cm (½-inch)

2 tablespoons fennel seeds

drizzle of olive oil

sea salt flakes and freshly ground black pepper

1 quantity of Mojo Verde (*see* page 42), to serve

Preheat the oven to 130°C fan (300°F), Gas Mark 2.

Put the soaked black beans in a casserole dish big enough to also hold the pork belly, along with the onion, garlic, rosemary, bay leaves, chipotle chillies, chopped tomatoes and chicken stock. Give everything a good stir.

Season the pork belly on both sides with salt, pepper and the fennel seeds. Lay the belly on top of the ingredients in the dish, skin side up, and drizzle with a little olive oil. Bake for 3 hours.

Meanwhile, make the mojo verde following the recipe on page 42, storing in the refrigerator until needed.

Once the 3 hours has passed, remove the pot from the oven and crank the oven temperature up to 220°C fan (475°F), Gas Mark 9.

When the oven has reached the set temperature, return the pot to the oven for 8–10 minutes to crisp up the pork skin. It will puff up, but do be careful as it can burn fairly quickly.

Remove the pot from the oven and let the pork rest for 30 minutes.

Lift the pork out and set aside while you check the seasoning of the beans, then cut the pork into slices about 2cm (¾-inch) thick. To serve, place a spoonful of mojo verde on each plate, add a spoonful of beans and lay the pork slices on top.

A meaty variation on the classic shakshuka, made with spicy merguez sausages that I cook at least once a week at home for the family. This works for breakfast, lunch and dinner!

Shakbanger!

olive oil, for cooking

4 merguez sausages

½ onion, finely chopped

2 garlic cloves, finely chopped

1 bay leaf

1 red chilli, finely chopped

1 teaspoon cumin seeds, toasted

1 teaspoon smoked paprika

pinch of cayenne pepper

1 red pepper, cored, deseeded and cut into slices 5mm (¼-inch) thick

400g (14oz) can of chopped tomatoes

200ml (7fl oz) vegetable stock

⅓ small bunch (about 10g/¼oz) coriander, leaves and stems finely chopped

⅓ small bunch (about 10g/¼oz) mint, leaves finely sliced

4 eggs

sea salt flakes and freshly ground black pepper

Pour a splash of olive oil in a medium saucepan over a medium heat and sear the sausages all over for about 5 minutes until nice and brown. Remove from the pan and set aside.

Add the onion, garlic, bay leaf and chilli to the pan and sauté together for 3 minutes – a little colour is OK. Season with salt and pepper.

Stir in the cumin, paprika and cayenne and cook for another 3 minutes. Then add the red pepper and cook for 5 minutes until it begins to soften.

Pour in the chopped tomatoes and the vegetable stock and bring to the boil, then reduce the heat and simmer for 10 minutes.

Return the sausages to the pan and simmer for 5 minutes more.

Stir in the coriander and mint. Crack the eggs into the pan in 4 little wells around the sausages and season with salt and pepper. Simmer over a very low heat for 10 minutes until the eggs are set but still soft. You may want to add a lid for the last 2 minutes to help set the tops of the eggs.

SERVES 4

Preparation time 15 minutes
Cooking time 2¾ hours

You can't beat a good hotpot, and with some Lebanese vibes going on, this classic is lifted to new heights.

Lebanese lamb hotpot

700g (1lb 9oz) boneless lamb neck, cut into 2cm (¾-inch) dice

2 tablespoons plain flour

vegetable oil, for cooking

1 onion, chopped

3 carrots, peeled and cut into 1cm (½-inch) dice

2 leeks, trimmed, cleaned, halved lengthways and cut into half-rounds 1cm (½-inch) thick

5 fluffy-textured potatoes, such as Maris Piper, peeled and cut into rounds 1cm (½-inch) thick

1 litre (1¾ pints) chicken stock

50ml (2fl oz) butter, melted

sea salt flakes and freshly ground black pepper

SPICE MIX

handful of coriander

2 garlic cloves, chopped

1 teaspoon ground cumin

1 teaspoon ground coriander

pinch of chilli flakes

1 teaspoon fennel seeds

1 teaspoon salt

juice of 1 lemon

4 tablespoons olive oil

Preheat the oven to 140°C fan (325°F), Gas Mark 3.

First, make the spice mix by blitzing all the ingredients together in a blender until smooth.

Next, toss the lamb neck pieces in the flour until evenly coated.

Heat a good splash of vegetable oil in a flameproof casserole dish over a medium heat and seal the lamb until coloured on all sides.

Pour in the spice mix, stir in well and cook for 3–4 minutes.

Stir in the onion, carrots and leeks and season with salt and pepper, then arrange the potato rounds on top, overlapping all the way around, starting on the outside and finishing in the middle.

Pour the chicken stock over – it should come up above the meat but just below the potatoes (have a peep to check by moving the centre potato slice). Brush the melted butter all over the top and season with salt and pepper.

Put a lid on the casserole and bake for 2 hours.

Remove from the oven, lift off the lid and increase the oven temperature to 170°C fan (375°F), Gas Mark 5.

Return the casserole to the oven for another 30 minutes until nicely coloured on top.

SERVES 4

Preparation time 10 minutes
Cooking time 30 minutes

A warming bowl of food to eat on your lap after a busy day. Quick, easy, nourishing and satisfying!

Sweet potato, black bean & chorizo chilli

vegetable oil, for cooking

250g (9oz) cooking chorizo sausages, skins removed and cut into 2cm (¾-inch) dice

1 onion, finely chopped

1 garlic clove, finely chopped

1 sprig of rosemary

1 teaspoon chilli powder

1 tablespoon smoked paprika

1 star anise

1 tablespoon ready-made chipotle chilli in adobo sauce

2 sweet potatoes, peeled and cut into 2cm (¾-inch) dice

400g (14oz) can of black beans, drained

500ml (18fl oz) vegetable stock

a few sprigs of coriander, leaves roughly chopped

2 tablespoons soured cream

20g (¾oz) Cheddar cheese, grated

sea salt flakes and freshly ground black pepper

Pour a splash of vegetable oil in a large saucepan over a medium heat. Add the chorizo, onion, garlic and rosemary and sauté for 7–8 minutes until the onion is soft but not coloured.

Next, add the chilli powder, smoked paprika, star anise and chipotle chilli and cook for 3 minutes. Season with salt and pepper.

Add the sweet potatoes and stir in well, then continue to sauté all the ingredients together for another 4 minutes.

Stir in the black beans, pour in the stock and bring to the boil, then reduce the heat and simmer for 15 minutes.

Stir in the coriander and check the seasoning. Remove the star anise and rosemary, then serve the chilli in bowls with a spoon of soured cream on top and the Cheddar sprinkled all over.

SERVES 2

Preparation time 30 minutes
Cooking time 1 hour

'Nduja is a spicy, spreadable salami from Calabria in Italy. It's a stunning ingredient that adds tons of flavour to a dish like this. If you can't get hold of it, cooking chorizo works well, too.

Hasselback potato, fennel & 'nduja tray bake

500g (1lb 2oz) new potatoes
1 fennel bulb, halved and cut into 2cm (¾-inch) pieces
2 sprigs of rosemary
1 tablespoon dried oregano
100ml (3½fl oz) olive oil
80g (2¾oz) 'nduja
10–12 cherry tomatoes
a few sprigs of basil, leaves picked
sea salt flakes and freshly ground black pepper

Preheat the oven to 170°C fan (375°F), Gas Mark 5.

Make a vertical cut across the width of each new potato every 2mm (1/16 inch) all the way along its length, cutting three-quarters of the way down through the potato. A good tip is to lay a wooden spoon either side of each potato to make sure you don't cut right through it.

Add the potatoes to a roasting tray big enough to hold all the ingredients, along with the fennel, rosemary, oregano and olive oil, and toss everything together with a little salt and pepper.

Roll the 'nduja into small cherry-sized balls and randomly scatter over, then roast for 30 minutes.

Give the contents of the tray a stir, then return to the oven for another 20 minutes.

After 20 minutes, stir once more and scatter the cherry tomatoes over, then return to the oven for a final 10 minutes.

Remove from the oven for the last time, sprinkle over the basil leaves and serve straight away.

Sides

Light and fresh, this would go perfectly with any barbecue, especially lamb.

Carrot & pistachio salad with orange & mint

3 carrots

50g (1¾oz) unsalted pistachios

juice of 1 orange

50ml (2fl oz) olive oil

a few sprigs of mint, leaves picked and roughly chopped

sea salt flakes and freshly ground black pepper

Peel the carrots, then grate them into a mixing bowl (use a julienne grater if you have one).

Toast the pistachios in a dry nonstick frying pan over a medium heat for 2–3 minutes, then let them cool.

Add the cooled pistachios to the carrots with the orange juice and olive oil.

Finely shred the mint and stir into the salad, then season with salt and pepper.

Preparation time 10 minutes
Cooking time 25 minutes

If the sun is shining, use the barbecue for this instead of the oven. It sits brilliantly alongside a steak or grilled chicken.

Roasted broccoli, garlic, yogurt & chilli

500g (1lb 2oz) Tenderstem broccoli

50ml (2fl oz) olive oil

juice of 1 lemon

2 tablespoons Greek yogurt

1 red chilli, finely sliced

20g (¾oz) butter

2 garlic cloves, finely sliced

sea salt flakes and freshly ground black pepper

Preheat the oven to 180°C fan (400°F), Gas Mark 6.

Put the broccoli and olive oil in a roasting tray, toss together and season with salt and pepper.

Roast for 15 minutes until the broccoli starts to colour and the stems feel almost cooked.

Meanwhile, mix the lemon juice into the yogurt and set aside.

Remove the tray from the oven, add the chilli and stir in, then roast for another 5 minutes.

While the broccoli finishes roasting, melt the butter in a nonstick frying pan over a medium heat, add the garlic slices and fry until golden brown.

Remove the tray from the oven, pour the garlic and the butter it was cooked in over the broccoli and give it a good toss, then spoon over the yogurt and serve.

When in season, use locally grown asparagus; it's one of the best ingredients around. I'd match this side to grilled fish.

Asparagus with spiced butter & roasted hazelnuts

50g (1¾oz) butter

1 teaspoon coriander seeds

1 star anise

1 bunch of asparagus, woody ends removed

20g (¾oz) blanched hazelnuts

sea salt flakes and freshly ground black pepper

Heat a nonstick frying pan over a medium heat. Add the butter, coriander seeds and star anise and cook for 3–4 minutes, taking care not to colour the butter.

Next, add the asparagus with the hazelnuts and season with salt and pepper.

Gently sauté the asparagus in the butter for 5–6 minutes until cooked but still with a crunch.

Lift the asparagus on to a plate and spoon the hazelnuts on top, then drizzle some of the butter around.

SERVES 2

Preparation time 10 minutes
Cooking time 15 minutes, plus cooling

I only like kale if it's drenched in butter or roasted/fried until crisp. This dish just looks like a load of roasted kale, but as you dig your spoon in, you get to a lovely, subtly spiced avocado yogurt beneath and the two go so well together.

Crispy kale, avocado & jalapeño yogurt

2 large handfuls of kale

50ml (2fl oz) olive oil

1 avocado, peeled and stoned

juice of 2 limes

1 jalapeño chilli, finely chopped

a few sprigs of coriander, leaves and stems finely chopped

2 tablespoons natural yogurt

sea salt flakes and freshly ground black pepper

Preheat an oven to 200°C fan (425°F), Gas Mark 7.

Dress the kale leaves with the olive oil and put in a roasting tray, then season with salt and pepper.

Roast for 12–15 minutes until the leaves become crisp.

Remove the kale from the oven and let it cool.

Put the avocado, lime juice, chilli, coriander and yogurt in a blender and blend together to make a thick dressing/purée. Season with salt and pepper.

Spoon the avocado mixture on to a plate, then cover with the crispy kale leaves.

SERVES 4

Preparation time 10 minutes
Cooking time 40 minutes

Harissa has an almost addictive flavour that works really well with the sweetness of the squash. A brilliant pairing with roast lamb or chicken.

Harissa-roasted butternut squash

1 butternut squash, peeled, deseeded and cut into 2cm (¾-inch) dice

2 sprigs of rosemary

1 tablespoon harissa paste

50ml (2fl oz) olive oil

sea salt flakes and freshly ground black pepper

Preheat an oven to 160°C fan (350°F), Gas Mark 4.

Put all the ingredients in a roasting tray, season with salt and pepper and give them a good mix.

Roast for 40 minutes.

Remove the tray from the oven and discard the rosemary before serving.

Preparation time 10 minutes
Cooking time 1 hour

A colourful and hearty vegetable roast with just a touch of honey to bring out the sweetness of the vegetables. This is great alongside a spiced lentil salad or to accompany a roast chicken.

Roasted roots with ricotta, sage & honey

2 raw beetroots, peeled and quartered

3 carrots, peeled and halved lengthways

2 parsnips, peeled and quartered

2 turnips, peeled and quartered

4 garlic cloves (unpeeled), bashed

50ml (2fl oz) olive oil

1 sprig of rosemary

20g (¾oz) butter

10–12 sage leaves

80g (2¾oz) ricotta cheese

2 tablespoons clear honey

sea salt flakes and freshly ground black pepper

Preheat the oven to 180°C fan (400°F), Gas Mark 6.

Put the root vegetables, garlic cloves, olive oil and rosemary in a large roasting tray and season with salt and pepper.

Toss all the ingredients together, then roast for 25 minutes until they begin to colour.

Remove the tray from the oven and cover with foil, then roast for another 45 minutes.

Meanwhile, heat a nonstick frying pan over a medium heat. Add the butter and, once it begins to colour, add the sage leaves and cook for 30–40 seconds until crisp.

Turn off the heat and set aside until the veggies are ready.

When they are ready, remove the tray from the oven, take off the foil and discard the rosemary and garlic.

Spoon over the ricotta in even dollops, then drizzle over the honey.

Scatter over the sage leaves and drizzle with the leftover sage-flavoured butter from the pan.

SERVES 2

Preparation time 5 minutes
Cooking time 10 minutes

Frying sprouts takes them to the next level; the texture of the crispy leaves is so nice. Serve alongside baked fish.

Fried Brussels sprouts with soy & orange

vegetable oil, for deep-frying

300g (10½oz) Brussels sprouts, quartered, outer leaves removed

SOY & ORANGE DRESSING

2 tablespoons orange juice

1 tablespoon fish sauce

1 tablespoon light soy sauce

2 tablespoons clear honey

1 tablespoon mirin

To make the dressing, bring all the ingredients to the boil in a saucepan and reduce to a honey-like consistency. Set aside to cool.

Heat the oil for deep-frying in a deep-fat fryer or a deep saucepan to 170°C (340°F). (If you don't have a jam thermometer, to test if the oil is hot enough, drop a sprout into the oil – if it sizzles immediately the oil is ready.) Carefully add the sprouts to the hot oil, in 2 batches, and fry for about 4 minutes until golden and crisp.

Remove with a slotted spoon straight on to kitchen paper to drain the excess oil.

Transfer the sprouts to a mixing bowl and drizzle 2–3 tablespoons of the dressing over while tossing so that they are evenly coated.

Cauliflowers are great flavour absorbers, so using lots of Indian spices here works really well. Serve alongside roast chicken or lamb.

Whole roast Indian-spiced cauliflower

1 large cauliflower, leaves removed

1 tablespoon Greek yogurt

3 sprigs of coriander, leaves roughly chopped

freshly ground black pepper

SPICED BUTTER

100g (3½oz) butter

3 garlic cloves, peeled

20g (¾oz) fresh root ginger, peeled

1 green chilli

a few sprigs of coriander, leaves finely chopped

1 tablespoon cumin seeds

1 tablespoon coriander seeds

1 tablespoon fennel seeds

1 teaspoon ground turmeric

1 teaspoon chilli flakes

seeds from 2 cardamom pods

sea salt flakes and freshly ground black pepper

Preheat an oven to 180°C fan (400°F), Gas Mark 6.

Put all the ingredients for the spiced butter in a blender and blitz together until smooth.

Add the cauliflower to a baking dish big enough to hold it and rub the butter all over. Season with salt and pepper.

Roast the cauliflower for 40 minutes, taking out to baste every 10 minutes.

When ready, remove the dish from the oven and lift the cauliflower out on to a plate. Cut it into quarters and separate slightly.

Spoon the yogurt on top and sprinkle the chopped coriander over. Finish by drizzling a little of the butter from the pot over and around the cauliflower and grind over black pepper to serve.

There's not much better than buttery Anna potatoes (or *pommes Anna*). They go with pretty much anything.

Spiced Anna potatoes

125g (4½oz) butter

pinch of saffron threads

1 teaspoon ground turmeric

1 tablespoon cumin seeds

1 tablespoon coriander seeds

3 cardamom pods

pinch of chilli flakes

6 fluffy-textured potatoes, such as Maris Piper

sea salt flakes and freshly ground black pepper

Preheat the oven to 170°C (375°F), Gas Mark 5.

Melt the butter with the spices in a saucepan over a low heat and let them infuse over the gentle heat for 10 minutes. Season with salt and pepper. The milk solids will separate, so skim them off and discard.

Strain the butter through a sieve and set aside.

Peel the potatoes, then use a mandolin to finely slice them 2mm (1/16-inch) thick.

Cover the base of an ovenproof nonstick frying pan, about 25cm (10-inches) in diameter, with a layer of the potato slices, overlapping them slightly.

Brush with the spiced butter, then repeat until you have used up all the potatoes. Reserve any remaining butter. Cover the pan with a lid and bake for 1½ hours.

Remove the pan from the oven, lift off the lid and press the potatoes down to form an even layer.

Increase the oven temperature to 200°C fan (425°F), Gas Mark 7.

Give the potatoes one last brush of the spiced butter, then bake for a final 30 minutes to colour and crisp the top.

Preparation time 5 minutes
Cooking time 25 minutes

Based on the classic *petit pois à la Française*, this is a brilliant dish to go with a roast chicken.

Braised Little Gems with peas & mint

30g (1oz) butter

1 onion, finely chopped

2 bay leaves

2 tablespoons plain flour

500ml (18fl oz) chicken stock

2 Little Gem lettuces, quartered

100g (3½oz) frozen peas

10 mint leaves, finely shredded

sea salt flakes and freshly ground black pepper

Melt the butter in a saucepan over a medium heat. Add the onion with the bay leaves and sweat for 4–5 minutes until softened but not coloured. Season with salt and pepper.

Remove and discard the bay leaves. Add the flour and stir in to make a slightly thin roux around the onion.

Gradually add the chicken stock while stirring constantly. Once all the stock is incorporated, bring to a simmer.

Add the Little Gem quarters and simmer for 12 minutes.

Stir in the peas and bring back to the boil, then check the seasoning. When ready, stir in the mint and serve.

Desserts

Preparation time 20 minutes,
plus resting
Cooking time 1 hour 25 minutes

This is perfect for a summer lunch dessert; berries and custard are a match made in heaven.

Summer berry custard tart

1 quantity of Sweet Pastry
(*see* page 228)

50g (1¾oz) blueberries

50g (1¾oz) strawberries, hulled and quartered

50g (1¾oz) blackberries

50g (1¾oz) raspberries

200ml (7fl oz) double cream

200ml (7fl oz) milk

2 vanilla pods, split in half lengthways

finely grated zest of 1 orange

finely grated zest of 1 lemon

8 egg yolks

100g (3½oz) caster sugar

Follow the recipe on page 228 to bake sweet pastry in a 20cm (8-inch) loose-bottomed tart tin.

Once you have removed the baked tart case from the oven and let it cool slightly at room temperature, arrange all the berries evenly in the tart case.

Put the cream, milk, vanilla pods and orange and lemon zest in a saucepan over a medium heat and bring to the boil.

In the meantime, whisk the egg yolks and sugar together in a mixing bowl until pale and fluffy.

Once the cream mixture has reached the boil, gradually pour it over the egg yolk mixture while still whisking.

Strain the custard through a sieve, then let it sit for a few minutes.

Skim off any froth from the custard, then carefully pour it over the berries all the way to the top of the tart case.

Carefully slide the tart into the oven and bake for 35 minutes until the custard is set but there is still a slight wobble in the centre.

Remove the tart from the oven and let it cool before serving.

This is one of my all-time favourite desserts. As soon as I smell this baking it makes me smile instantly. I bake this all year round, changing the fruits with the seasons.

Blackberry & almond tart

200g (7oz) butter, softened, plus extra for greasing

200g (7oz) caster sugar

2 eggs

200g (7oz) ground almonds

320g (11½oz) sheet of ready-rolled sweet shortcrust pastry

about 30 (250g/9oz) blackberries

50g (1¾oz) flaked almonds

clotted cream, to serve

Preheat the oven to 160°C fan (350°F), Gas Mark 4. Grease a 23cm (9-inch) loose-bottomed tart tin with butter, then put on to a baking sheet lined with baking parchment.

To make the frangipane, cream the butter and sugar together in a mixing bowl until pale.

Slowly beat in the eggs, then fold in the ground almonds.

Drape the sheet of pastry over the greased tin and press down around the sides so that it's a snug fit, leaving an overhang of a few centimetres all round. Place a sheet of baking parchment on top of the pastry and fill the pastry case with dried or baking beans or uncooked rice.

Bake until the exposed edges start to turn golden – this should take about 15 minutes.

Remove from the oven, lift out the paper and beans, then bake for another 10 minutes until the base is golden brown, too.

Remove the tart case from the oven, spoon the frangipane mixture into the tart case and spread it out evenly. Arrange the blackberries evenly on top, pressing them down slightly so that they are half in and half out of the frangipane, then scatter the flaked almonds all over.

Bake for 40 minutes until the frangipane is set and golden.

Remove the baked tart from the oven, then carefully trim off the excess pastry from the edges. Let the tart cool before taking out of the tin. Serve at room temperature with a good spoon of clotted cream.

Preparation time 10 minutes
Cooking time 50 minutes

This is an impressive-looking cake that's really easy to make. Great on its own and even better with a scoop of vanilla ice cream.

Pear & ginger upside-down cake

100g (3½oz) butter, softened, plus extra for greasing

100g (3½oz) plain flour

100g (3½oz) light brown sugar

½ teaspoon baking powder

2 eggs

1 vanilla pod

½ teaspoon ground ginger

¼ teaspoon ground cinnamon

6 pieces of stem ginger, cut into 5mm (¼-inch) dice

CARAMEL PEARS

2–3 ripe, soft pears

225g (8oz) caster sugar

55g (2oz) butter, chopped

Grease a 20cm (8-inch) cake tin with butter and set aside.

First make the caramel pears. Peel the pears and cut into quarters, removing the core, then slice into wedges 1cm (½-inch) thick. Arrange in a fan over the base of the cake tin.

To make the caramel, put the sugar in a saucepan and add a splash of cold water, then give it a little mix. Use a wet pastry brush to clean the sides of the pan of any sugar crystals (which will otherwise cause the caramel to crystallize), then cook slowly over a low heat until the sugar melts and turns to a golden brown caramel.

Remove from the heat and add the butter gradually, stirring all the time.

Pour the caramel over the pears evenly and set aside while you make the cake batter.

Preheat an oven to 180°C fan (400°F), Gas Mark 6.

Place all the cake ingredients in a mixing bowl and whisk together until smooth.

Pour the cake batter over the caramel pears, then bake for 35 minutes or until a skewer inserted into the middle comes out clean.

Remove the cake from the oven and leave to cool for 10 minutes in the tin before carefully turning out on to a plate. Serve warm.

SERVES 8

Preparation time 20 minutes
Cooking time 1 hour

This cake has lots of autumnal flavours but is really light – the perfect way to end a rich meal.

Ricotta cake with figs & orange blossom custard

butter, for greasing

500g (1lb 2oz) ricotta cheese

4 eggs, separated

seeds from 1 vanilla pod

30g (1oz) plain flour

250g (9oz) caster sugar

finely grated zest of 2 lemons

6 figs, cut lengthways into slices 5mm (¼-inch) thick

CUSTARD

225ml (8fl oz) milk

225ml (8fl oz) double cream

3 egg yolks

45g (1½oz) sugar

50ml (2fl oz) orange blossom water

Preheat an oven to 160°C fan (350°F), Gas Mark 4. Grease a 20cm (8-inch) cake tin with butter.

To make the cake, whisk together the ricotta, egg yolks and vanilla seeds in a mixing bowl. Add the flour, sugar and lemon zest and mix until combined.

In another bowl, whisk the egg whites until stiff, then fold them into the cake batter.

Pour the cake batter into the greased cake tin, then cover the surface with the fig slices, overlapping a little. Bake for 50 minutes–1 hour until just firm in the centre.

Remove the cake from the oven and let it cool completely in the tin.

To make the custard, pour the milk and cream into a saucepan, place over a medium heat and bring to the boil.

Meanwhile, whisk the egg yolks and sugar together in a mixing bowl until pale and fluffy.

Once the cream mixture has reached the boil, gradually pour it over the egg yolk mixture while still whisking. Add the orange blossom water, then pour the mixture into the pan and cook over a low heat, stirring constantly, until it thickens, taking care not to scramble the eggs. Remove from the heat and pass the custard through a sieve.

Serve the custard, hot or cold, poured over the ricotta cake.

Baking custard makes for a really indulgent, thick consistency, which I just love.

Baked saffron custards with strawberries & cream

500ml (18fl oz) double cream

2 pinches of saffron threads

4 egg yolks

50g (1¾oz) caster sugar

40g (1½oz) icing sugar, sifted

seeds from 2 vanilla pods

12 strawberries, to serve

Preheat an oven to 100°C fan (250°F), Gas Mark ½.

To make the custard, pour 150ml (5fl oz) of the cream into a saucepan, add the saffron and bring to the boil over a medium heat.

Meanwhile, mix the egg yolks and caster sugar together in a mixing bowl just until blended.

Once the cream has reached the boil, gradually pour it over the egg yolk mixture while still whisking.

Pour into 4 x 150ml (5fl-oz) ramekins and stand on a baking sheet. Bake for 30 minutes.

Remove the custards from the oven and leave them to cool to room temperature.

To make the vanilla cream, whisk the remaining cream, icing sugar and vanilla seeds together in a mixing bowl until soft peaks form. Cover and refrigerate until ready to serve.

Cut the strawberries in either half or quarters, depending on their size.

To serve, arrange the strawberries on the custards and add a good spoon of the vanilla cream on top.

SERVES 4

Preparation time 20 minutes,
plus chilling
Cooking time 15 minutes

This is a good one to knock up in advance; the curd benefits from the extra resting time in the refrigerator.

Blood orange curd with chestnut & vanilla shortbread

CURD

200g (7oz) caster sugar

100g (3½oz) butter

finely grated zest and juice of
2 blood oranges

finely grated zest and juice of 1 lemon

4 eggs

SHORTBREAD

125g (4½oz) butter, chopped

55g (2oz) sugar, plus extra (optional)
for sprinkling

100g (3½oz) plain flour

80g (2¾oz) chestnut flour

seeds from 1 vanilla pod

To make the curd, put all the ingredients in a heatproof mixing bowl set over a pan of simmering water (being careful not to let the base of the bowl touch the water) and keep whisking for 4–5 minutes until thickened – do keep an eye on it so that it doesn't curdle.

Divide between 4 little pots and put in the refrigerator to firm up while you make the shortbread.

To make the shortbread, crumble all the ingredients together with your fingertips in a mixing bowl, then bring together to form a dough.

Roll out the dough until 1cm (½-inch) thick, then cut into fingers about 3 x 8cm (1¼ x 3¼-inches), which is a good size to dunk into the curd. Transfer to a baking sheet lined with baking parchment. Gather any trimmings together and repeat the process so that there isn't any waste.

Pop in the refrigerator for 30 minutes to firm up.

Meanwhile, preheat an oven to 160°C fan (350°F), Gas Mark 4.

Remove the baking sheet from the refrigerator and prick each shortbread lightly with a fork. Bake for 10 minutes until golden.

If using, sprinkle with sugar as soon as they come out of the oven, then let them cool on the baking sheet. Serve each pot of curd with a few shortbread fingers on the side. Store any leftover shortbread in an airtight container for 2–3 days.

SERVES 4

Preparation time 5 minutes
Cooking time 1 hour 10 minutes

I love rice pudding; it brings back lots of nostalgic memories for me. I serve it here with rhubarb to keep it light and not too sweet, but mango would be great, too.

Coconut rice pudding with poached rhubarb

RICE PUDDING

100g (3½oz) pudding rice

230ml (8¼fl oz) coconut milk

250ml (9fl oz) milk

2 tablespoons caster sugar

finely grated zest of 1 orange

1 vanilla pod, split in half lengthways

RHUBARB

3 rhubarb sticks, peeled and cut into 3cm (1¼-inch) pieces

1 tablespoon caster sugar

juice of 1 orange

30g (1oz) unsweetened dried coconut flakes, toasted, to serve

Preheat the oven to 160°C fan (350°F), Gas Mark 4.

Put all the ingredients for the rice pudding in a large saucepan and bring to the boil.

Pour into an ovenproof dish and place a sheet of baking parchment on top. Bake for 1 hour, removing the baking paper for the last 20 minutes.

Meanwhile, to cook the rhubarb, put it in a saucepan with the sugar and orange juice. Place a piece of baking parchment on top and bring to a simmer over a low heat. Cook for 5–6 minutes until the rhubarb starts to break down.

Turn off the heat and let the rhubarb cool a little.

Serve the rice pudding in bowls with a good spoon of rhubarb and a sprinkle of coconut flakes.

I love making hybrid desserts and this one is a winner. The Amaretto in the custard really ramps up the almond flavour, and the crunchy flaked almonds on top finish it off nicely.

Crème brûlée Bakewell tart

SWEET PASTRY

200g (7oz) plain flour, sifted, plus extra for dusting

100g (3½oz) butter, softened, plus extra for greasing

80g (2¾oz) icing sugar, sifted

seeds from 1 vanilla pod

2 egg yolks, plus 2 more to glaze

CRÈME BRÛLÉE

400ml (14fl oz) double cream

100ml (3½fl oz) milk

50ml (2fl oz) Amaretto

1 vanilla pod, split in half lengthways

5 egg yolks

50g (1¾oz) caster sugar

TO FINISH

100g (3½oz) cherry jam

50g (1¾oz) flaked almonds

3 tablespoons caster sugar

First, make the sweet pastry. Put the flour into a large mixing bowl and make a well in the middle. Add the butter, icing sugar and vanilla seeds to the well and use your fingers to massage into the flour to make a crumbly dough.

Add the egg yolks and continue to work until a smooth dough is formed. Wrap in clingfilm and put in the refrigerator for 30 minutes to rest and firm up.

Next, make the crème brûlée mixture. Put the cream, milk, Amaretto and vanilla pod in a saucepan over a medium heat and heat to just below boiling point.

Meanwhile, whisk the egg yolks and sugar together in a large bowl until well mixed and a little pale.

Once the cream mixture is just coming to the boil, gradually pour it over the egg yolk mixture while still whisking and continue to whisk for another minute. Lift out the vanilla pod and set the mixture aside.

Grease a 23cm (9-inch) loose-bottomed tart tin or dish about 5cm (2-inches) deep.

Take the chilled pastry from the refrigerator and roll out on a lightly floured work surface into a roughly shaped round 2mm (¹⁄₁₆-inch) thick. Drape the pastry over the greased tart tin and press down around the sides so that it's a snug fit, leaving an overhang of a few centimetres all round. Return the pastry case to the refrigerator for 30 minutes to rest again.

Preheat the oven to 170°C fan (375°F), Gas Mark 5.

Remove the pastry case from the refrigerator. Place a sheet of baking parchment on top of the pastry and fill the pastry case with dried or baking beans or uncooked rice. Bake for 25 minutes until the exposed edges just start to colour.

Continued over the page…

Remove from the oven and lift out the paper and beans. Using a fork, prick some holes in the pastry base and bake for another 15 minutes.

Meanwhile, beat the egg yolks for glazing with a splash of water.

Remove the tart case from the oven and brush all over with the egg wash. Pop back in the oven for a final 5 minutes, then remove and let it cool a bit at room temperature. Reduce the oven temperature to 160°C fan (350°F), Gas Mark 4.

Spread the jam over the base of the pastry, then pour in the crème brûlée mixture. Bake for 45 minutes until set – there should still be a very slight wobble to the centre.

Remove the tart from the oven and leave to cool for a few minutes in the tin. Once cooled but still warm, sprinkle over the caster sugar, then, using a blowtorch, caramelize the top. If you don't have a blowtorch, place under the grill to caramelize, but keep an eye on it so it doesn't burn. As soon as the sugar starts bubbling, scatter the flaked almonds over so they stick to the surface.

Carefully trim off the excess pastry from the edges, then let the tart sit for a few minutes for the sugar to set and turn nice and crunchy.

A fresh, summery light recipe that takes hardly any time to make. You can change the fruit as the seasons evolve, too.

Peach & basil Eton mess

200ml (7fl oz) double cream

40g (1½oz) icing sugar, sifted

2 meringue nests

1 ripe peach, stoned, peeled and cut into wedges

a sprig of basil, leaves finely shredded

1 tablespoon Amaretto

1 chunk of white chocolate, for grating

Whip the cream together with the icing sugar in a mixing bowl until soft peaks form. Crumble in the meringue nests and fold in.

In another bowl, stir the peaches, basil and Amaretto together.

To serve, put a good spoonful of the meringue mixture in each serving bowl and divide the peaches on top. Finish with a grating of white chocolate.

Preparation time 20 minutes,
plus chilling overnight
Cooking time 5 minutes

This recipe for a set cheesecake has a wonderful savoury flavour that comes from the salted caramel and brown butter. I've always preferred set cheesecake to the richer baked ones; they seem much lighter and less food-coma inducing!

Brown butter cheesecake

BASE

250g (9oz) oat style biscuits
(I use Hobnobs)

100g (3½oz) butter, melted

30g (1oz) honey

FILLING

80g (3½oz) butter

600g (1lb 5oz) cream cheese

80g (2¾oz) icing sugar, sifted

40g (1½oz) honey

seeds from 1 vanilla pod

100g (3½oz) ricotta cheese

100ml (3½fl oz) double cream

4 tablespoons Salted Caramel Sauce
(*see* page 240)

To make the cheesecake base, blitz the biscuits, melted butter and honey together in a food processor.

Press into the base of a 20cm (8-inch) springform cake tin.

To make the cheesecake filling, melt the butter in a saucepan over a medium heat, then continue to cook for about 4 minutes until it becomes brown and smells nutty, being careful not to let it burn. Take the pan off the heat and set aside.

Beat the cream cheese with the icing sugar, honey and vanilla seeds in a large mixing bowl.

Add the ricotta and cream, then pour in the brown butter, mixing well.

Pour the mixture into the cake tin on top of the biscuit base, then put in the refrigerator overnight to set. When ready to serve, remove the cheesecake from the tin on to a serving plate and drizzle over the salted caramel sauce.

Preparation time 15 minutes,
plus chilling
Cooking time 5 minutes

This brings back so many memories for me of being a kid and eating Angel Delight or Instant Whip. I can picture myself licking the bowl as a 6-year-old as if it were yesterday.

Nostalgic butterscotch mousse

80g (2¾oz) light muscovado sugar

50ml (2fl oz) spiced rum

50g (1¾oz) butter

seeds of 1 vanilla pod

2 eggs, separated

200ml (7fl oz) double cream, plus 100ml (3½fl oz) to serve

1 tablespoon caster sugar

Put the muscovado sugar, rum, butter and vanilla seeds in a saucepan over a medium heat and stir until the sugar has dissolved. Remove from the heat.

Whisk the egg yolks in a mixing bowl until pale, then slowly add the hot sugar and butter mixture while still whisking. Continue to whisk for 5 minutes.

Whisk the cream and the egg whites in 2 separate mixing bowls until soft peaks form.

Fold the whisked egg whites into the egg yolk mixture, then add the cream and carefully fold in.

Spoon the mousse into 4 serving glasses and chill in the refrigerator for at least 3 hours. Serve with a little double cream poured over each, if you like.

A chiffon cake is very light and also easy to make. If using a traditional chiffon cake tin, it looks quite spectacular, but if you don't have one, then a normal cake tin is totally fine.

Salted caramel chocolate chiffon cake

butter, for greasing
6 eggs, separated
50g (1¾oz) cocoa powder, sifted
125ml (4fl oz) vegetable oil
seeds from 1 vanilla pod
350g (12oz) caster sugar
200ml (7fl oz) water
250g (9oz) plain flour, sifted
1 teaspoon bicarbonate of soda
pinch of sea salt flakes

BUTTERCREAM
250g (9oz) soft light brown sugar
150ml (5fl oz) double cream
½ teaspoon sea salt flakes
140g (5oz) butter, softened

ITALIAN MERINGUE
225g (8oz) caster sugar
150ml (5fl oz) water
90g (3¼oz) egg whites

To make the cake, preheat the oven to 160°C fan (350°F), Gas Mark 4. Grease a chiffon cake tin, or regular 22cm (8½-inch) round cake tin, with butter.

Put the egg yolks, cocoa powder, vegetable oil, vanilla seeds and sugar in a mixing bowl and whisk together until smooth, then whisk in the water.

Add the flour, bicarbonate of soda and salt and mix together.

In another mixing bowl, whisk the 6 egg whites until stiff, then fold into the cake batter.

Pour the cake batter into the prepared tin and bake for 50 minutes or until a skewer inserted into the middle comes out clean. Remove the cake from the oven and turn out on to a wire rack to cool.

To make the buttercream, put the brown sugar, cream and salt in a saucepan over a medium heat and heat, stirring, until the sugar has dissolved. Cook for a further 3 minutes, then remove from the heat and let the cream cool.

Using a stand mixer fitted with the paddle attachment, beat the butter until pale and smooth. Add the cooled cream and mix in well. Scrape into a bowl and clean out the stand mixer bowl.

To make the Italian meringue, put the sugar in a pan and gently pour over the water. Use a wet pastry brush to clean the sides of the pan of any sugar crystals (which will otherwise cause the caramel to crystallize), then heat over a medium heat.

Meanwhile, using a stand mixer, start whisking the egg whites on a slow speed. Once the sugar has reached 116°C (240°F) on a sugar thermometer, increase the speed of whisking the egg whites until soft peaks form. Continue to heat the sugar until it reaches 121°C (250°F), at which point slowly pour it into the egg whites while still whisking on a high speed. When the sugar syrup has all been added, continue to whisk until the meringue mixture has cooled to room temperature.

Transfer the meringue mixture to a piping bag fitted with a star nozzle.

Slice the cake horizontally into 3 layers and "butter" the middle 2 layers with the buttercream. Sandwich back together, then finish the cake by piping the meringue on top in small peaks.

Use a cooks' blowtorch to colour the top of the peaks, then the cake is ready to go.

Preparation time 20 minutes
Cooking time 25 minutes

This recipe was made and tweaked so many times by Becs because she was obsessed with making the perfect brownie. I hadn't noticed that she added her name to the title when making changes to the recipe... which is fair enough considering how often she made them!

Becs' triple chocolate & caramel brownies

150g (5½oz) butter, plus extra for greasing

130g (4¾oz) dark chocolate (70% cocoa solids), broken into small pieces

275g (9¾oz) caster sugar

seeds from 1 vanilla pod, or ½ teaspoon vanilla bean paste

3 eggs

100g (3½oz) plain flour, sifted

50g (1¾oz) milk chocolate chips

50g (1¾oz) white chocolate chips

60g (2¼oz) cocoa powder, sifted

100g (3½oz) canned condensed milk caramel (such as Carnation)

pinch of sea salt flakes (optional)

Preheat the oven to 180°C fan (400°F), Gas Mark 6. Grease and line a shallow baking tin, 30 x 15cm (12 x 6 inches), with greaseproof paper.

Melt the chocolate and butter together either in a microwave or in a heatproof mixing bowl set over a pan of simmering water (being careful not to let the base of the bowl touch the water), stirring often.

In another mixing bowl, whisk the sugar, vanilla and eggs together until pale and fluffy.

Add the melted chocolate and butter mixture to the egg mixture and fold in.

Fold in the flour and cocoa powder, then all the chocolate chips.

Pour half the brownie mixture into the lined baking tin and then, using a teaspoon, dollop on half the caramel. Pour over the remaining brownie mixture, then dollop on the rest of the caramel. Using a knife, swirl the caramel into the brownie mixture.

Bake for 20–22 minutes – there should be no wobble, but it will still look a little undercooked, which is perfect.

Remove from the oven and sprinkle the sea salt over at the end, if you like. Let the brownie cool completely in the tin before lifting out and cutting into 12 pieces. They keep really well for a few days in an airtight container.

Preparation time 20 minutes,
plus chilling
Cooking time 10 minutes

The simplicity of a great chocolate mousse combined with a rich, slightly salted caramel is a tough one to beat. This is a perfect recipe if you're entertaining; all the work is done in advance.

Chocolate mousse with salted caramel

250g (9oz) dark chocolate (70% cocoa solids), broken into small pieces

4 eggs, separated

65g (2¼oz) golden caster sugar

1 tablespoon cocoa powder

SALTED CARAMEL SAUCE

70g (2½oz) golden caster sugar

25g (1oz) butter, chopped

140ml (5fl oz) double cream

pinch of sea salt flakes

Melt the chocolate either in a microwave or in a heatproof mixing bowl set over a pan of simmering water (being careful not to let the base of the bowl touch the water), stirring often.

Whisk the egg whites in a mixing bowl until stiff, while gradually adding the sugar.

In another mixing bowl, whisk the yolks and the cocoa powder together, then whisk the mixture into the chocolate (which should be melted but not too hot).

Next, fold in the whisked egg whites, taking care not to knock out the air.

Spoon into 4 small glasses or ramekins and put in the refrigerator for at least 3 hours to set.

To make the caramel sauce, put the sugar in a saucepan and cook slowly over a low heat until it dissolves and turns golden. Continue to cook until it becomes caramel coloured.

Remove from the heat and add the butter gradually, stirring all the time.

Next, stir in the cream and salt, then let the sauce cool.

To serve, drizzle a good spoon of the salted caramel sauce over each ramekin of mousse to cover the top.

These are great on their own or with a scoop of ice cream. I love the addition of salt and sesame to bring a slightly savoury taste to them.

White chocolate & tahini blondies

125g (4½oz) unsalted butter, plus extra for greasing

220g (7¾oz) soft light brown sugar

30g (1oz) white tahini

1 egg

seeds from 1 vanilla pod

pinch of sea salt flakes

140g (5oz) plain flour

100g (3½oz) white chocolate chips

20g (¾oz) black sesame seeds

20g (¾oz) white sesame seeds

Preheat the oven to 170°C fan (375°F), Gas Mark 5. Line a shallow baking tin, about 20 x 10cm (8 x 4 inches), with buttered greaseproof paper.

Put the butter, sugar and tahini in a mixing bowl and mix together until blended.

Add the egg, vanilla seeds and salt and mix together well, then add the flour and mix until well incorporated. Stir in the chocolate chips.

Spread the mixture evenly over the base of the lined baking tin, then sprinkle the black and white sesame seeds on top.

Bake for 30 minutes.

Remove from the oven and let the blondies cool completely in the tin before lifting out and cutting into portions.

Seasonal menus
Spring

After a long winter, the coming of spring brings so much feel-good factor. The parks burst back into life and the produce in the markets is so refreshing. We can finally leave the robust cooking of winter behind and celebrate some fantastic vegetables, cooking and eating in a much lighter way.

STARTER

Asparagus with buttermilk & roasted almonds
(*see* page 68)

MAIN

Baked cod with wild garlic pesto, new potatoes
& peas (*see* page 125)

DESSERT

Crème brûlée Bakewell tart
(*see* page 228)

Summer

Summer is all about cooking and eating in the garden for us, for every meal of the day (weather permitting, which, admittedly, can be very tricky to plan).

Colourful feasts, grilled fish and meats, fresh salads using the brilliant vegetables and stone fruits on offer and long, lazy lunches in the sun are the first things I think of when summer is here, and we always make sure we take full advantage of the season.

That means using the barbecue as much as possible. Anything needing the oven will be made ahead in the morning so that we can all stay together outside rather than running back indoors every few minutes. That works for the blackberry tart below, but also for slow-cooked meats that can be cooked ahead of time and then finished on the barbecue. Entertaining is about being with your guests and relaxed, so the more prep you can do, the better. If not using a barbecue, a griddle pan on the hob is fine.

STARTER

Peperonata bruschetta with ricotta (*see* page 74)

MAIN

Herby lamb leg steaks with Israeli couscous & grilled peaches (*see* page 108)

DESSERT

Peach & basil Eton mess (*see* page 231)

Autumn

As the leaves begin to fall and the temperature drops, autumn is the signal that the food is about to get a whole lot more comforting. In much the same way as I look forward to the lightness of spring and the colourful, tasty food of summer, I always get excited by the prospect of autumn, too. Wild mushrooms, Jerusalem artichokes and figs hint at warmer cooking, preparing us for the winter ahead.

STARTER

Parsnip soup with garlic butter mushrooms
& chives (*see* page 71)

MAIN

Slow-roast pork belly with Jerusalem artichoke
& pearl barley risotto (*see* page 118)

DESSERT

Ricotta cake with figs & orange blossom custard
(*see* page 221)

Winter

This is the time of year when we truly embrace the warming flavours of winter; slow-cooked meats and red wine in front of the fire, comforting ourselves in the face of the often miserable weather. The winter can be long, so using food to cheer myself and others up is an obvious antidote for me. There's something lovely about it being cold outside and spending a day in the kitchen. The aromas your loved one inhales when they walk in the door – it's worth it just for that.

STARTER

Crab claws roasted in garlic butter (*see* page 93)

MAIN

Slow-cooked treacle ox cheek with celeriac dauphinoise & nutty crumble (*see* page 117)

DESSERT

Blood orange curd with chestnut & vanilla shortbread (*see* page 225)

Index

UK–US glossary

UK	US
Aubergine	Eggplant
Baking paper	Parchment paper
Bicarbonate of soda	Baking soda
Bird's eye chilli	Thai chili pepper
Biscuits, oat-style	Plain oatmeal cookies
Black treacle	Blackstrap molasses
Broccoli	Broccolini
Butter bean	Lima bean
Caster sugar	Superfine sugar
Chicory	Belgian endive
Clingfilm	Plastic wrap
Cocktail stick	Toothpick
Coriander	Cilantro
Cornflour	Cornstarch
Courgette	Zucchini
Crisps	Potato chips
Crumble	Crumb topping
Double cream	Heavy cream
Flaked almonds	Silvered almonds
Griddle	Grill (verb) on a stove or BBQ, ridged grill pan (noun)
Grill	Broiler (noun), broil (verb); see also griddle
Groundnut oil	Peanut oil
Hob	Stove
Icing sugar	Confectioners' sugar, also known as powdered sugar
Kitchen paper	Paper towels
Knob (of butter)	Pat (of butter)
Minced meat	Ground meat
Lardons	Small strips of fatty meat such as bacon or pancetta
Pak choi	Bok choy
Passata	Tomato puree
Plain flour	All-purpose flour
Prawns	Shrimp
Pudding rice	Short-grain rice
Rasher	Slice (of bacon)
Rocket	Arugula
Runner beans	Green beans
Self-raising flour	Substitute with all-purpose flour plus 1 tsp baking powder per 125 g (1 cup) flour (unlike US self-rising flour, the UK version does not contain salt)
Single cream	Light cream
Smoked haddock	Finnan Haddie; can use cod, flounder, or sole instead
Spring onion	Scallion
Stone(d)	Pit(ted)
Streaky bacon	regular bacon
Steaks: fillet	tenderloin
rump	sirloin
sirloin	strip
Strong white flour	White bread flour
Sushi rice	Glutinous rice
Wild garlic	Ramps

Author's acknowledgements

Thanks to all the wonderful people who helped book number three come to life. Opening the pub in the same year made this a particularly challenging time, so my thanks are twofold: firstly, to everyone involved in creating this book, and secondly, to everyone who had to deal with me at peak tiredness – Becs and Tilly predominantly…

To our mates whose dinners or gatherings I couldn't go to or cancelled… sorry!

Thank you to everyone at Octopus for believing in this book and working with me again to make it happen, especially Alison, Sybella and Juliette.

To Dan, Aloha, Natalie, Linda and everyone on the shoot for all your hard work and excellence to make the food look as good as it tastes.

To Becs, for eating all the brownies and kindly changing the name… what would this book be without your willingness to test…?

And last, but by no means least, Holly, my agent, and, most importantly, a friend who I trust implicitly and without whom I would be lost – thank you.